Transforming Emotional Pain

Transforming Emotional Pain presents an accessible self-help approach to mental health based on Emotion-Focused Therapy (EFT).

Based on the principles of EFT, and developed by clinicians and researchers, this client-focused workbook is designed to supplement psychotherapy and can also serve as a self-help book. It will help readers learn how to regulate feelings that are unpleasant and transform painful feelings, so that they can fulfil their needs and feel more connected and empowered in their lives. Providing a step-by-step sequential guide to exploring, embracing, and transforming emotions, the various chapters guide the reader to help overcome emotional avoidance, with sections on: transforming the emotional self-interrupter; transforming the inner self-worrier; transforming the self-critic; and healing from emotional injury.

This workbook can be used by trained therapists, mental health professionals, psychology professionals, and trainees as supplementary to their therapeutic interventions with clients. It can also be used by general readers with an interest in self-help literature and resources or anyone wanting to explore, embrace, and transform their emotions.

Aman Kwatra, DCounsPsych, is Consultant Psychologist and Research Associate at Spectrum.Life. His main professional and research interests are in leveraging digital technologies for the provision and advancement of mental health services.

Ladislav Timulak, PhD, is Professor in Counselling Psychology at Trinity College Dublin, Ireland. His main research interest is psychotherapy research, particularly the development of emotion-focused therapy.

Sharon Lu Huixian, DClinPsych, is a Principal Clinical Psychologist at the Institute of Mental Health, Singapore. Her main research interests are in the implementation and dissemination of internet-delivered interventions and psychotherapy outcomes research.

Ciara Joyce, DClinPsych, is a Clinical Psychologist at the Student Counselling Service in Trinity College Dublin, Ireland. She is interested in the promotion of mental health and social change.

Mary Creaner, DPsych, is an Assistant Professor with the Doctorate in Counselling Psychology and Director of the MSc in Clinical Supervision, Trinity College Dublin, Ireland.

Transforming Emotional Pain

An Emotion-Focused Workbook

Aman Kwatra, Ladislav Timulak,
Sharon Lu Huixian, Ciara Joyce
and Mary Creaner

Routledge
Taylor & Francis Group

LONDON AND NEW YORK

Cover image: © Getty Images

First published 2023
by Routledge
4 Park Square, Milton Park, Abingdon, Oxon OX14 4RN

and by Routledge
605 Third Avenue, New York, NY 10158

Routledge is an imprint of the Taylor & Francis Group, an informa business

British Library Cataloguing-in-Publication Data
A catalogue record for this book is available from the British Library

Library of Congress Cataloging-in-Publication Data
Names: Kwatra, Aman, author. | Timulak, Ladislav, author. | Huixian, Sharon Lu, author. | Joyce, Ciara, author. | Creaner, Mary, author.
Title: Transforming emotional pain : an emotion-focused workbook / Aman Kwatra, Ladislav Timulak, Sharon Lu Huixian, Ciara Joyce, Mary Creaner.
Description: Abingdon, Oxon ; New York, NY : Routledge, 2022. | Includes bibliographical references and index. |
Identifiers: LCCN 2022021016 (print) | LCCN 2022021017 (ebook) | ISBN 9781032063515 (hbk) | ISBN 9781032063393 (pbk) | ISBN 9781003201861 (ebk)
Subjects: LCSH: Emotion-focused therapy. | Psychotherapy. | Mental health.
Classification: LCC RC489.F62 K83 2022 (print) | LCC RC489.F62 (ebook) | DDC 616.89/14--dc23/eng/20220629
LC record available at https://lccn.loc.gov/2022021016
LC ebook record available at https://lccn.loc.gov/2022021017

ISBN: 978-1-032-06351-5 (hbk)
ISBN: 978-1-032-06339-3 (pbk)
ISBN: 978-1-003-20186-1 (ebk)

DOI: 10.4324/9781003201861

Typeset in Times New Roman
by KnowledgeWorks Global Ltd.

Access the Support Material: www.routledge.com/9781032063393

Contents

About the Authors

Aman Kwatra, DCounsPsych, is a Consultant Psychologist and Research Associate at Spectrum.Life. His main professional and research interests are in leveraging digital technologies for the provision and advancement of mental health services and in recovery from complex trauma. Aman completed his MSc in Psychology at University of St. Andrews, Scotland, and attained his Doctorate in Counselling Psychology at Trinity College Dublin, Ireland. He has previously worked with the Irish Prison Service and has a background in Post-War Recovery Studies (University of York) and International Relations (University of Bristol).

Ladislav Timulak, PhD, is Professor in Counselling Psychology at Trinity College Dublin, Ireland. Ladislav (or short Laco; read Latso) is involved in the training of counselling psychologists and various psychotherapy trainings in Ireland and internationally. His main research interest is psychotherapy research, particularly the development of emotion-focused therapy. He is currently developing this form of therapy as a transdiagnostic treatment for depression, anxiety, and related disorders. He has written eight books, over 100 peer reviewed papers and chapters in both his native language, Slovak, and in English. His most recent books include *Transforming Emotional Pain in Psychotherapy: An Emotion-Focused Approach* (Routledge, 2015), *Transforming Generalized Anxiety: An Emotion-Focused Approach* (with co-author James McElvaney; Routledge, 2017), and *Essentials of Descriptive-Interpretive Qualitative Research* (with Robert Elliott) and *Transdiagnostic Emotion-Focused Therapy* (with co-author Daragh Keogh) both published by the American Psychological Association (2021). He serves on various editorial boards. He maintains a part-time private practice.

Sharon Lu Huixian, DClinPsych, is a Principal Clinical Psychologist at the Institute of Mental Health, Singapore. She completed her clinical training in Macquarie University, Sydney. She has over a decade of experience in providing outpatient and inpatient psychological services to a wide range of clinical disorders ranging from depression, anxiety to schizophrenia and those with interpersonal conflicts. She regularly conducts clinical supervision, clinical training and research. She also worked as an Adjunct Associate Professor in the Department of Psychology in the National University of Singapore. Sharon has a keen interest in the delivery of internet-based treatments to reduce treatment barriers, deliberate practice to improve therapeutic expertise in therapists and maternal mental health. Her recent publication (with colleagues) includes: 'A Randomised Controlled Trial of Clinician-Guided Internet-Based Cognitive Behavioural Therapy for Depressed

Patients in Singapore', *Frontiers in Psychology* (2021). She is also a co-editor of a book on Mind This Voice Series: *The Write to Recovery*, which is a collection of clients' narratives through the road of struggles and recovery.

Ciara Joyce, DClinPsych, is a Clinical Psychologist and Student Counsellor at Trinity College Dublin, Ireland. She completed her clinical training in the United Kingdom at Lancaster University with the National Health Service (NHS), and she is a chartered member of the Psychological Society of Ireland (PSI). Ciara has experience working therapeutically across the lifespan, using an integrative perspective of person-centered, compassion, and emotion-focused approaches. Her research interests include better understanding the collective power structures that affect mental health and exploring the use of particular therapeutic modalities to improve individual wellbeing. Her professional interests involve working therapeutically with individuals and groups, providing training and supervision, and disseminating knowledge to empower social change. Publications include: 'Beyond the Revolving Door: A Narrative Enquiry Into the Long-Term Lived Experience of Eating Disorders', *Qualitative Health Research* (2019) and a co-authored chapter on 'Modelling Imperfection and Developing the Imperfect Self' in Parry, S. (Eds) *Sharing Compassion: Self-Care and Resilience in Clinical Practice* (2017). Jessica Kingsley Publishers.

Mary Creaner, DPsych, is an Assistant Professor and Research Coordinator with the Doctorate in Counselling Psychology and Director of the M.Sc. in Clinical Supervision, Trinity College Dublin, Ireland. Having commenced her career in education, Mary subsequently qualified as a psychotherapist and clinical supervisor and has been involved in developing and delivering a variety of adult education courses and professional development training in this area for over 25 years. She is an accredited therapist and clinical supervisor with the Irish Association for Counselling and Psychotherapy (IACP), and a member of the American Psychological Association (APA). Among her recent publications is a chapter on the *Role of Social Media in Counselling and Psychotherapy* in R. Tribe and J. Morrissey (Eds.) *Handbook of Professional and Ethical Issues for Psychologists, Counsellors, and Psychotherapists* (3rd ed., Routledge, 2020). Mary's research interests include clinical supervision, adult learning, and psychotherapy research and she presents her research nationally and internationally.

Disclaimer

This workbook is based on Emotion-Focused Therapy, which is an evidence-based psychological approach. However, please note that none of the authors take responsibility for any possible consequences from any treatment, procedure, task, exercise, or action taken by any person reading or following the information in this book. The publication of this book does not constitute the practice of medicine or psychotherapy. This workbook does not attempt to replace or substitute for medical or professional advice, diagnosis, treatment, or any other instructions from your doctor, qualified psychological or other health professional. The authors advise the reader to check with a doctor, psychologist, or other qualified professional before undertaking any course of treatment regarding any matters related to your own health or situation or if you have specific questions in this regard.

Please note that the guidance and strategies are intended as self-help and may not be suitable for your situation. You should, where necessary, consult with an appropriate qualified professional. The authors shall not be liable for any loss or profit or any commercial damages, including but not limited to special, incidental, consequential, or other damages. Case examples referred in this book are generic and based on collective representation. No relation to any specific person is either implied or intended.

Acknowledgements

We would like to sincerely thank everyone who made this workbook possible. We offer appreciation to Les Greenberg and other early developers of Emotion-Focused Therapy such as Robert Elliott, Laura Rice, Jeanne Watson, Rhonda Goldman, and many more colleagues around the world. We extend our thanks to Hayley Bell for piloting this programme and to all those who participated. A special word of gratitude to Katarina Timulakova for providing valuable feedback and suggestions throughout the process. Finally, many thanks to Joanne Forshaw, Grace McDonnell, Daradi Patar, Emily Boyd, and everyone in the editorial and production teams at Routledge.

Glossary

Experiencer   This a part of ourselves impacted by our self-critic, self-worrier, or self-interrupter, etc. We referred to this part of ourselves in the chair dialogue tasks (such as Self-Critic, Self-Worrier, Self-Interrupter). It is the part where we feel the cost of the problematic (self) treatment and it is the part where we articulate what we need.

Real-Play   This is the term we use for describing the tasks that we are suggesting for you to engage in. We call them real-play rather than role-play as you are bringing to them your real experiences.

Self-Critic   This is a part of us that is critical of ourselves by highlighting our shortcomings, and evaluating ourselves very harshly. In an adaptive form it is a part of us that wants to better us (self-adjust), wants us to meet our standards. Unfortunately, this process often turns out to be less adaptive and turns into problematic self-criticism.

Self-Interrupter   This is a part of us that wants to stop us from feeling (painful) emotions, or wants us to stop expressing feelings, the expression of which is scary for us, or it is a part of us that stops us from getting into situations that could evoke painful emotions in us. The interruption protects us but it also cuts us off from important and valuable experiences.

Self-Worrier   This is a part of us that produces worries. We self-worry by mentally engaging with potential scenarios that could evoke painful feelings. In this way, we want to prepare ourselves for those potential scenarios, however, it leaves us feeling anxious.

Introduction to the Transforming Emotional Pain Workbook

Learning Goals

1 To gain an overview of the background, purpose, and structure of the workbook and gain insights into how the course presented in this workbook can be used for helping you to tolerate and transform painful emotions.
2 To introduce the various chapters of the workbook and highlight important things to remember before beginning the course.

Introduction

Welcome to the *Transforming Emotional Pain* workbook. This workbook is designed to support people who want to be more in touch with their emotions, who want to be informed by their emotions, who want to be able to stay with their emotions, and who want to transform particularly painful emotions into new more fulfilling and enriching emotional experiences. By picking up this book you have already made a commitment to your overall wellbeing and have taken an important step in learning how to 'connect with', 'be informed by', and if needed, 'transform' your emotions.

This workbook is based on the theoretical principles of Emotion-Focused Therapy (EFT). EFT is an evidence-based psychological intervention that has been developed and derived from a long history and tradition of humanistic therapies (e.g., person-centred therapy and Gestalt therapy). Since its development (for instance, see the works of Greenberg et al., 1993; Elliott et al. 2004; Greenberg, 2015; Greenberg, 2017), EFT has been extensively researched and has gained a strong body of evidence supporting its effectiveness. It has also become very popular amongst practitioners. This programme is based on the work of EFT theorists stated already (e.g., Greenberg et al. 1993; Elliott et al. 2004) and specifically on the principles conceptualized and presented in the works of Timulak (2015), Timulak and McElvaney (2018), and Timulak and Keogh (2022). It has been developed by clinicians and researchers to ensure you have access to the most up-to-date, evidence-based approaches to learning more about the value and role of emotions in our lives.

The purpose of this workbook is to provide you with important psychological experiences and knowledge that can empower you to better understand the role that emotions play in your life, so that you can *be informed by what they are trying to say to you* and *transform them if necessary*. Emotions tell us whether our needs (for closeness, connection, recognition, validation, safety) are being met in our life. Emotions thus contain important information about our wellbeing in the world, particularly in the

DOI: 10.4324/9781003201861-1

interaction with other people around us. Therefore, *instead of avoiding* emotions or trying to get rid of them, we hope that you will be able to embrace them and *use them* to *inform and guide* your choices and actions in life.

To this end, the workbook offers information as well as various experiential tasks that you can use to strengthen your capacity to attend to emotions, differentiate between them, articulate the needs to which the emotions point, and eventually transform the emotions that keep you stuck in the pain that is too much or too difficult to be with. These tasks are self-explorative in nature and can be undertaken with minimal additional resources. Essentially, all you need to work through this workbook is a pen and a notebook, two empty chairs, and a quiet place where you can work through the tasks without being interrupted. You can go through this workbook on your own or as a supplement to emotion-focused therapy. [*To find qualified EFT therapists in your country, please see the list on the website of the International Society for Emotion-Focused Therapy* (www.iseft.org).]

An Emotion-Focused Approach

Emotions tell us what is important for us and whether our emotional needs are being fulfilled. They tell us whether we feel connected with our close ones, whether we are valued by the people whose opinions matter to us, or whether we feel safe in the world. We all want to have pleasant feelings and avoid unpleasant feelings. However, avoiding or disconnecting from unpleasant feelings can lead to more distress down the line as we are no longer in a position to listen to what these important feelings have to tell us. The main goal of EFT is to get a sense about what emotions are telling us in terms of our needs. Thereafter, we can start to find ways of intentionally meeting those needs within ourselves, in the relationships with people around us, and in pursuing our life projects. Therefore, the key focus of this workbook is to help you learn how to *access* your emotions, how to be able to *stay* with and *transform* them if needed so that you can carry on with things that feel difficult and live your life safely, fully, and connected to people around you.

About this Workbook

This workbook is designed to be followed over at least eight weeks duration but can be followed for a much longer period or you can return to it as needed once you finish it. It is a practical and experiential tasks-based workbook. As you progress through this workbook, you will be encouraged to work through each chapter within a guided but flexible time period. Some chapters may also recommend repeated practice of certain important tasks. Additionally, each chapter will contain content and tools that have been designed to help you engage with the materials learnt and to reflect on their specific relevance for your own life. To make this workbook as easy to follow as possible, we have provided you with examples of how to complete the tasks, by tracing the journey of two composite participants (i.e., hypothetical examples that are based on our experiences of people with various difficulties), as they progress through this workbook alongside your own journey. Examples of how these two participants (we call them **Timothy** and **Alice**) engage with the various activities offered in this workbook are contained in the appropriate chapter appendices. The first example follows the experience of Timothy and the second follows the experience of Alice. See Boxes 0.1 and 0.2. for more information about the two examples.

Box 0.1

Case Example: Timothy

Timothy is a 27-year-old gym instructor who shares a house with three of his friends. He recently broke up with his girlfriend of two years because she wanted him to move in with her, which he didn't feel ready for. Timothy has been feeling quite low since the break-up. His friend who he works with in the gym has expressed concern for him after he showed up late for work on a couple of occasions. Timothy values his job at the gym as it is a role that he feels he is good at, and somewhere he feels he belongs. He found not working during the Covid-19 pandemic to be especially difficult and ended up putting on some weight. He is frustrated that his mood has started to impact this aspect of his life. He worries about having hurt his ex-girlfriend's feelings and that he is letting the gym down.

Timothy would describe himself as quite a shy person. He has also struggled with his confidence over the years having experienced bullying from a young age in school. Timothy's mother is Black, and his father is White, and there were no other students of similar background in the primary school he attended. Halfway through primary school, when Timothy was 7, his dad moved away for work and his parents separated shortly afterwards. This was a real blow for Timothy and although he still saw his father every second weekend, he felt hurt and confused by his decision to leave. He wondered if it was his fault that his parents had separated. Timothy has always been very close to his mother and enjoys spending time with her. Growing up she worked long hours as a nurse and it was important for him to help her out around the house. He moved out after finishing college but still lives nearby.

Timothy tried to work hard throughout his time in school, but he struggled with dyslexia, so by the time Timothy started secondary school he felt like a bit of a failure and was a loner. There were a few multicultural and multi-ethnic students in the school he attended but none had separated parents like him. He has always felt like he has stood out for all the wrong reasons, and still feels like he doesn't belong. When he travels to visit his mother's extended family he feels like the outsider. Even when he spends time with his dad, he continues to feel like an outsider. This makes him even worry that people will think he is adopted. Timothy's mum encouraged him to get involved in sports at school and that is where Timothy started to excel and make friends. He met his ex-girlfriend, Rachel, on a night out. She was his first girlfriend, and he cares about her a lot, but he is scared to commit to being with her forever. He felt that they were too different and that he would only end up holding her back.

Course Overview and Summary

An emotion-focused approach may be different from other therapeutic approaches that you may have previously tried. However, the experiential tasks that you will find in this workbook are quite straightforward and with some regular practice, you can quickly get familiar with them. The course itself is divided into seven chapters. A description of each of the chapters and their main aims are included in the following sections, and a brief overview and summary is also provided in Table 0.1. The chapters in this workbook have been designed to be reviewed in the order they are presented here, however, if there is a particular chapter that captures your attention, feel free to review it out of turn.

Box 0.2

Case Example: Alice

Alice is a 47-year-old part-time sales manager who lives with her husband of 16 years, her 12-year-old son and her mother-in-law. She decided to speak to her family doctor about her mood after talking to her husband who shared with her that he noticed that her mood has been more irritable and would often snap at him and their son over trivial issues. For example, she raised her voice when her son forgot to bring his wallet to school and she felt very guilty about it afterwards. Alice also reported that she has difficulties going to sleep at night and often wakes up at 4 or 5 am in the mornings and cannot return to sleep again. During the Covid-19 pandemic, she avoided social gatherings due to her fear of the virus and it has been difficult for her to rekindle her interest in social activities since. She also lost interest in her hobbies such as yoga and having meals with her friends.

Alice described herself as a perfectionistic person who tends to drive herself quite hard to excel in whatever she does. She switched to part-time work two years ago, so that she could spend more time tutoring her son who is struggling in school. She is stressed about preparing her son for his primary school leaving examinations this year. She struggles with self-critical thoughts such as, "*I am so weak and can't handle stress as well as the other working moms*". Additionally, her mother-in-law had a fall last year and her husband decided to move her to their house so that he can take care of her. Tensions with her mother-in-law mainly arise from Alice perceiving her mother-in-law to be critical of her parenting practices.

Alice grew up in a family where her parents were not emotionally expressive and mainly showed their love through providing for their children's physical needs. Alice has one younger brother, and she often thinks that her parents loved him more than her because males were traditionally favoured over females in her extended family/community. Her parents were also very strict with her and held high expectations of her to take care of her younger brother and to be a good role model to him.

Table 0.1 Overview of the Workbook

Chapter 1: The Role of Emotions in Our Lives
This chapter focuses on how our emotions provide information about our relationships, and our emotional needs.
Chapter 2: Optimal Use of Emotions
This chapter focuses on how to connect with your emotions and how to tolerate them when they feel overwhelming.
Chapter 3: Overcoming Emotional Avoidance (The Self-Interrupter)
This chapter looks at the main ways in which we try and protect ourselves from difficult feelings by stopping them or avoiding situations that could trigger them.
Chapter 4: Overcoming Emotional Avoidance (The Self-Worrier)
This chapter builds on the progress made in the previous chapter and focuses on how we worry about potential situations that could trigger emotional pain.
Chapter 5: Transforming the Self-Critic
This chapter aims at making us more aware of the ways in which we often criticize ourselves unhelpfully, particularly in the context of emotionally demanding situations.
Chapter 6: Transforming Interpersonal Emotional Injury (Unfinished Business)
This chapter focuses on how to transform and heal interpersonal emotional injuries.
Chapter 7: Summary and Conclusion
This chapter focuses on consolidating the learning from this workbook. It also provides you with additional resources that could be helpful for you in your journey ahead.

Chapter 1: The Role of Emotions in Our Lives

You will begin the course presented in this workbook with the first chapter focusing on how our emotions act as messengers that provide us with important information about our relationships, and our emotional needs. This chapter presents the concept of emotional pain. In this chapter you will look at the relationship of symptoms of anxiety and depression and more central emotional vulnerability we may experience that we refer to as core emotional pain (or core pain). You will learn about the core painful emotions that tend to be at the centre of human emotional suffering and emotional needs embedded in those painful emotions. You will be invited to reflect on the kinds of situations that often trigger painful emotions and take a closer look at how you treat yourself in the context of those triggering situations.

Several short tasks will be presented in this chapter for you to learn how to differentiate between your emotions, between the more symptomatic ones (like depression and anxiety) and the more underlying ones which are central and at the core of your experiences, like loneliness/sadness, shame, and fear. The tasks will be focused on recognizing the triggers of emotional pain as well as the problematic ways of how you may relate to yourself in the context of those triggers.

Chapter 2: Optimal Use of Emotions

This chapter will introduce you to important ways to connect with and stay with your emotions when they feel overwhelming. It will offer two experiential tasks, the Clearing a Space task and the Compassionate Self-Soothing task. Both tasks can be quite useful at times when you are feeling particularly upset or overwhelmed by an emotional experience. This chapter will form the foundation for your subsequent experiential work on the course (in the later chapters), and you can always return to the two tasks introduced in this chapter to regulate your emotions if upset or if your emotions feel too intense.

Chapter 3: Overcoming Emotional Avoidance (The Self-Interrupter)

This chapter will build on the previous chapter and will focus on helping you become more aware of how we can be emotionally avoidant. The chapter will offer an experiential task focused on emotional *interruption (or self-interruption)* (i.e., the ways we (a) stop ourselves from feeling painful or uncomfortable emotions, (b) stop expression of certain emotions in certain contexts, and (c) how we avoid situations that could trigger painful emotions). The task and the overall chapter should be able to assist you to feel and express important emotional experiences that inform your actions and behaviour.

Chapter 4: Overcoming Emotional Avoidance (The Self-Worrier)

In this chapter we will investigate how we try to protect ourselves from difficult feelings by engaging with potential scenarios in our thinking which may evoke anxiety. Our main focus in this chapter will be on assessing how *self-worrying* prepares us for potentially emotionally difficult situations, but how at the same time it triggers anxiety and keeps us on edge and tired. We will introduce an experiential task called

Overcoming the Self-Worrier that should help you to be more aware of how you worry yourself and consider the cost of that worrying. It will also help you to rebalance the worrying in such a way that it brings less anxiety.

Chapter 5: Transforming the Self-Critic

Chapter 5 will focus on helping you become more aware of the many ways we criticize ourselves and the adverse impact such criticism has on us. We often criticize ourselves in unhelpful ways, particularly when we face emotionally demanding situations which can further compound our experience of such situations. The core aim of this chapter is to introduce a transformational experiential task that will assist you in transforming your experience of *self-criticism* by being more aware of it, being able to see its impact, and being able to articulate what you may need in the face of such criticism. In doing so you will learn how to look after yourself when you are being impacted by the self-criticism and learn to set boundaries with the Self-Critic.

Chapter 6: Transforming Interpersonal Emotional Injury (Unfinished Business)

This chapter focuses on how to transform and heal the interpersonal emotional injuries that you may have experienced in relationships. It explores how many triggers of our core emotional pain often stem from previous difficult or challenging interactions with other people, especially when such interactions happened during developmentally sensitive times, but also at any time if they are particularly painful. Repeated or prolonged painful experiences often result in deeply entrenched emotional injuries that adversely affect many aspects of our present lives. In this chapter, we will gradually learn to work through such *emotional injuries*, so you can stay with vulnerable and painful feelings, be able to articulate what you need from yourself or from others, and learn how to have these needs or vulnerabilities responded to and recognized.

Chapter 7: Summary and Conclusion

This final chapter focuses on consolidating your learning by summarizing the key ideas and concepts from all chapters. It also provides you with additional resources that could be helpful for you in your journey ahead.

Before You Begin: 11 Key Points to Remember

1 Please remember that it is important to take your time when working through the chapters and undertaking the tasks. Don't feel rushed to do all the tasks together or to complete a full chapter in one sitting. Each chapter suggests the amount of time that would be required to work through the tasks, but this is only for guidance and is flexible. Please feel free to adjust the time to suit your own needs.

2 As the course focuses on working through your emotions, slight hesitation/ uncertainty when undertaking some of the more emotionally intense tasks is normal. Please go at your own pace and feel free to select only those situations to work on that you are comfortable with.

3 When undertaking the tasks remember to focus on your feelings and don't worry about the thoughts. Remember, this course focuses on emotions, so try not to get too caught up with thoughts or judgements.

4 The workbook introduces tasks that will require you to have conversations with different parts of an imagined self or with another imagined person. You will be seated on one chair and the imagined other will be thought of as sitting on another chair, facing you. Some people may find such tasks awkward and 'a bit weird' (e.g., when talking to an imagined self on another chair). This is normal and the feeling usually goes away when there is more familiarity with the tasks.

5 Redoing the experiential tasks is beneficial, so feel free to undertake any of them several times, as per your own comfort and need. Such repeated experience can go a long way in helping you internalize the process, and this can lead to optimizing the overall benefits that can be gained from the course. Also, each doing of the task brings a new learning.

6 The tasks listed in Chapter 2 (i.e., Clearing a Space and Compassionate Self-Soothing) have all been designed to help in soothing distressing emotions. Remember to return to these tasks whenever you need to.

7 The tasks are generally short in the amount of time required to complete them. However, since they deal with your emotions and working through potentially challenging past experiences, it is important to provide yourself with some private time and safe surroundings. Please ensure that you can undertake the tasks with minimal distractions and interruptions.

8 The key to the course is to proceed through it gently and gradually. Begin working with emotional situations that are not too painful or overwhelming; especially while you are still familiarizing yourself with the chapters and tasks. Thereafter, based on your own comfort, readiness, and desire, you can proceed to using the tasks to work through more challenging emotional experiences.

9 Please remember, as we mentioned, you can go through this workbook on your own or as a supplement to emotion-focused therapy. To find EFT therapists in your country, please see the list on the website of the International Society for Emotion-Focused Therapy (www.iseft.org). You may also decide to reach out to a friend for support. While you can undertake the tasks on your own or with an accredited therapist you might also find it helpful to talk to about the general process with a friend, perhaps even one who is following the workbook themselves!

10 Remember that there are completed examples of all tasks that you can refer to in the appendices. These can be helpful in providing more information about what you are required to do in the tasks, especially if anything seems unclear.

11 Finally, please note that you can download copies of all Task Worksheets and Guidance Sheets from the Support Material at: www.routledge.com/9781032063393.

We are very pleased that you have chosen to take this emotion-focused step in learning to effectively befriend and (if needed) transform your emotional experiences. We sincerely hope that this workbook supports you in this journey and guides you in your quest to enhance your life.

Chapter 1

The Role of Emotions in Our Lives

Learning Goals

1 To learn about the role of emotions in our lives.
2 To understand how emotions tell us whether our needs are being met.
3 To explore various situations that trigger different types of emotional responses and understand how we may treat ourselves in the context of such triggers.

Suggested duration: Two weeks

Introduction

Emotions tell us how we are when we go about our day to day lives. Emotions tell us whether our needs are being met or not, and help us clarify what is important for us to focus on. Essentially, emotions provide us with information about how well we are getting on in our relationships and our pursuits. Emotions are also the means by which we communicate quickly and directly with others, wherein our expressions, our body language, and our emotionally driven behaviours promptly convey to others what is going on for us and how we are feeling in any given situation.

This chapter will inform you about the different types of typical painful chronic emotions that we may experience and will also outline the *needs* embedded in those emotions. The chapter will also explore the various kinds of situations that often trigger painful emotional responses within us and then take a look at how we treat ourselves in the context of those triggers/situations. In doing so, the chapter will help you begin your journey in learning about how to *befriend the feelings* that are too intense and how to *transform* feelings that are too painful to lead to constructive actions.

Understanding Emotions and Emotional Pain

Emotions are diverse internal experiences that we all go through every day. They can vary in the intensity of their impact on people and can be experienced as pleasant or unpleasant. In this way, *emotional pain* can be described as an unpleasant, intense, overwhelming, and upsetting internal experience.

DOI: 10.4324/9781003201861-2

Symptoms of Emotional Pain

Emotional pain presents itself most typically in the form of symptoms of depression, anxiety, and irritability, or most commonly, a combination of these symptoms. We can feel hopeless, helpless, have low mood, we can be anxiously expecting danger, or we can be irritable with close ones or people around us. We can experience a mixture of confusing, upsetting, tormenting, and overwhelming thoughts and feelings. These are typically accompanied by unpleasant physiological experiences. For instance, in the form of an experience of tension in the middle parts of the body: such as in the throat, neck, shoulders, solar plexus, and in the stomach. We may also experience difficulties in breathing, muscular tensions, negatively functioning digestive system. We may experience poor sleep, low levels of energy, body aches, and low or very high levels of appetite, etc.

To understand more comprehensively why we suffer and experience emotional pain, it is important to understand what we seek in our lives and what matters to us. Learning from our clients in therapy we know that a portion of what brings distress is when we do not feel safe. We want to feel safe and want to avoid experiencing harm, both in the immediate present and also in the long term. Emotions provide us with vital information in this regard. For instance, anxiety informs us about the possible dangers that may be present which could be fatal or harmful to us. This is why sometimes when we experience a traumatic event in our lives, we can subsequently develop deeply ingrained apprehensive anxiety about the possibility of future trauma. Therefore, we fear any potential pain that could resemble such experienced trauma and we can become fearful of any situation that reminds us of the original traumatic situation in some way. This can lead to avoidant behaviour on our part.

Another aspect which characterizes the suffering that clients seeking help in therapy go through are experiences of loneliness, chronic sadness, and loss. Their antidotes, experiences of love and connection, are not only pleasurable to us, but they also provide us with security. Experiences of closeness and caring are thus antidotes to many scary aspects of life. The opposite of love, care, and connection is loneliness, chronic sadness, and loss. Loneliness, chronic sadness, and loss point to unmet needs for connection, closeness, enjoyment of the company of the other, etc. Chronic loneliness, sadness, and loss can lead to psychological withdrawal and physiological resignation. Loneliness can have several negative consequences on our physical and mental health. It can also prompt us to adopt maladaptive self-soothing behaviours, such as substance use, which tend to be counterproductive in the long term.

Another aspect of painful emotional experiences that clients present with in therapy relates to the lack of validation, appreciation, or acknowledgement. Validation brings us a sense of recognition and provides us with an identity-giving sense of the unique contribution we are making to others around us. A lack of appreciation, recognition, and acknowledgement or experiences of rejection evoke feelings of shame and its variants. In fact, experienced rejection can even hurt physically as the neural circuitry of emotional and physical pain is shared and gets activated when we feel rejected by others. Such experiences may lead us to withdraw from others socially, physically, and physiologically. We may feel irritable and hostile in return.

Painful experiences get encoded in our memory and colour how we are in the world. They shape how we see and experience our living and our interaction with others. Specific events that brought particularly painful emotional experiences impact how we experience similar situations in the future. Consequently, events of intrusion, danger that brought experiences of fear or events of loss, exclusion that led to experiences of loneliness or events of judgement and rejection that brought experiences of shame may be particularly pivotal. These situations not only bring us emotional injuries, but they also impact our functioning. These events impact how we experience and perceive our interaction with our environment, and with other people in the future. These painful experiences may also lead us to avoid situations that could bring similar painful experiences. In the context of triggers (situations, events) that bring us emotional pain we can also treat ourselves in a way that may compound the impact of these triggers. For instance, we can blame ourselves for how we were in those events, we can over-worry ourselves in terms of the similar future events, we can try to numb ourselves, to stop feeling anything so that we avoid pain, etc.

In this chapter we will begin by looking at how we understand emotional pain. You will engage in six tasks aimed at deepening your understanding of your personal painful emotional experience. These tasks are designed to be completed over two weeks, and the suggested duration is as follows:

Suggested Tasks for Week 1:

1   We will look at how we can differentiate between the Symptom Level Distress and the Underlying Core of our Emotional Pain.
2   We will guide you to look at your personal Core Emotional Pain.
3   We will guide you to reflect on the Situations that Trigger your Emotional Pain.

Suggested Tasks for Week 2:

4   We will look at the Avoidance Strategies you may engage in so as not to feel Emotional Pain.
5   We will look at how you Treat Yourself in the context of problematic triggers/ situations that may not be helpful for you.
6   We will guide you to reflect on particular Emotional Injuries that may have had a lasting impact on you.

Note: Remember that you do not need to undertake all the following tasks at one time or in one sitting. Please feel free to attend to these tasks in your own time. The duration is only a suggested guidance and can be adjusted to suit your individual needs.

Task 1: Understanding Symptomatic Distress and Underlying Vulnerability

When we encounter difficult situations, we may experience problematic emotional responses such as depression and/or anxiety. Depression may show in feelings of hopelessness, helplessness, feeling resigned to, a profound sense of overall sadness, and in some cases also in experiences of irritability, anger, or even a combination of these emotions. On the other hand, anxiety may show in feelings of panic, agitation, restlessness, worry, having physical pains and aches, nausea, tensions, and/or a sense of surrealness (i.e., feeling like you are not fully present in your own body). Both depression and anxiety have a similar function in mental health to a fever when we have a physical illness. These symptoms tell us that something is not quite right, without necessarily telling us what might be wrong. Typically, what is not quite right is that there are some other specific (underlying) feelings that are tied to a specific situation (or situations). These underlying feelings also point to potentially unmet needs that we had in those situations.

For instance, a person may have a general sense of frustration and irritation towards their romantic partner, while underneath this sense they may be responding to the fact that their romantic partner did not pay attention to them when they needed support after a difficult day at work. In this case the underlying feeling could be sadness that their partner was not there for them in a way that they needed. In this case, the underlying sadness may indicate that the person needed to feel connected to and supported by their partner. Consider another example, wherein a person may be anxious and apprehensive about an impending meeting with their employer at work. Here the underlying feeling could be humiliation/shame because they doubt their own competence and fear that their employer may criticize them. This underlying humiliation may indicate that they need to feel accepted and valued.

Now, please reflect on times when you may have felt down or anxious, emotions that may indicate for you (or may have historically indicated for you) that something is not quite right. In the following task (see Boxes 1.1 to 1.6), consider what emotional needs of yours may not have been met in a specific situation and how these may have contributed to your experience of feeling depressed or anxious. Space has been provided for you to write down these thoughts and experiences directly in this book. However, if you prefer, you can also download and print the required task worksheets from the Support Material (www.routledge.com/9781032063393) and complete the worksheets instead.

Note: Remember that you do not need to undertake all the following tasks at one time or in one sitting. Please feel free to attend to these tasks in your own time. You can always look up the completed examples from this chapter for Timothy and Alice in Appendix I (pages 133–157) if you need further guidance, clarification, or reference about how to undertake the task.

Considering Symptoms of Depression

Box 1.1

Reflecting on Symptoms of Depression

Symptoms of Depression

Reflect on a few unpleasant or distressing emotions and the accompanying situations which trigger these emotions. These could be depression like symptoms (e.g., feeling hopelessness, helplessness, resignation, feeling down, sad about everything, irritated, and/or feeling angry). Write these in the space provided here. *For example: I felt irritated/ resigned when my partner did not pay attention to me. (Use as much space as you need.)*

_____

_____

_____

_____

_____

_____

Box 1.2

Reflecting on Underlying Feelings in Depression

Underlying Feelings

Our unmet emotional needs bring emotional reactions (i.e., underlying feelings [e.g., feelings of disappointment, humiliation, embarrassment, or fear]) that we may feel *before* we get depressed. What are some of the underlying emotional reactions that you experienced in important emotional situations *before* you felt depressed? Please write in the space provided. *For example: I felt sadness that my partner was not interested in what upset me. (Use as much space as you need.)*

_____

_____

_____

_____

_____

_____

_____

Box 1.3

Reflecting on Unmet Needs (Depression)

Unmet Needs

Now reflect on the unmet emotional needs you may have had in such situations (e.g., need to be close, supported, valued, protected, etc.) that were not met. Please write them here in the space provided. *For example: my need was to be comforted by my partner. (Use as much space as you need.)*

_____

_____

_____

_____

_____

_____

Note: Remember that you do not need to undertake all the following tasks at one time or in one sitting. Please feel free to attend to these tasks in your own time.

Considering Symptoms of Anxiety

Box 1.4

Reflecting on Symptoms of Anxiety

Symptoms of Anxiety

Try to reflect on feelings of anxiety (e.g., nervousness, tension, hypervigilance) that you may have felt in *advance* of a situation that may potentially bring painful feelings. Please write them in the space provided. *For example: I feel anxious ahead of the meeting with my line manager. (Use as much space as you need.)*

_____

_____

_____

_____

_____

_____

_____

_____

Box 1.5

Reflecting on Underlying Feelings in Anxiety

Underlying Feelings of Anxiety (i.e., what you were dreading)

Anxiety tells us that we are dreading some situations and are fearful of the feelings that these situations may bring. What feelings would be difficult to feel in the situations you are dreading. These may, for instance, include feelings of being rejected, feeling alone, feeling not valued, feeling unprotected, or feeling scared. Please write them in the space provided. *For example: feeling humiliated by seeming incompetent in front of my line manager. (Use as much space as you need.)*

_____

_____

_____

_____

_____

_____

_____

_____

Box 1.6

Reflecting on Unmet Needs (Anxiety)

Unmet Needs

What emotional needs do these feelings point to? For instance, these may include needs such as the need to be accepted, to be safe, to be appreciated, to be cared for. Please write them in the space provided. *For example: I would want to be acknowledged by my line manager. (Use as much space as you need.)*

_____

_____

_____

_____

_____

_____

Task 2: Understanding Core Emotional Pain

Research on people's experience of attending therapy has found three main clusters of core emotional sensitivities. These are (1) the Sadness/Loneliness cluster, (2) the Shame cluster, and (3) the Fear (or Terror) cluster (see Table 1.1). People's experience of emotional suffering can therefore be categorized into one of these clusters. Each of these clusters relates to specific types of unmet emotional needs.

In this task (see Boxes 1.7 to 1.12), reflect on feelings of sadness/loneliness, shame and fear, and also reflect on corresponding underlying needs related to these feelings. Space has been provided for you to write down these thoughts and experiences directly in this book. As before, you can also download and print the required task worksheets from the Support Material (www.routledge.com/9781032063393) and complete the worksheets instead.

Note: Remember that you do not need to undertake all the following tasks at one time or in one sitting. You can also look up the completed examples of Timothy and Alice in Appendix I (pages 133–157). Please feel free to attend to these tasks in your own time.

Table 1.1 Examples of Core Painful Emotions and Associated Needs

Emotion Cluster	Examples	Related Unmet Need
Sadness/ Loneliness	Experiences of feeling alone, missing loved ones, feeling sad, missing love or connectedness and such related feelings, etc.	Need to be loved by, feeling love for someone, or feeling closely connected with others, etc.
Shame	Feeling humiliated, embarrassed, inadequate, flawed, worthless, etc.	Need to be accepted, valued, recognized, etc.
Fear/Terror	Feeling scared, panicky, unprotected, terrified, unsafe, etc.	Need to feel safe, protected, and secure, etc.

Considering the Sadness/Loneliness Cluster

Box 1.7

Reflecting on Feelings of Sadness/Loneliness

Sadness/Loneliness Cluster (Feelings)

Now try to reflect on your own emotional vulnerabilities and sensitivities. Which of these seem to belong to the 'Sadness/Loneliness' cluster (e.g., feeling alone, missing loved ones, feeling sad, missing love or connection and similar feelings)? Please write them in the space provided. *(Use as much space as you need.)*

Box 1.8

Reflecting on Unmet Needs in Sadness and Loneliness

Sadness/Loneliness Cluster (Unmet Emotional Needs)

Now please try to reflect on the corresponding emotional needs (e.g., longing for connection, love, closeness, and so on) that those emotions may be connected to. Please write them in the space provided. *(Use as much space as you need.)*

Note: Remember that you do not need to undertake all the following tasks at one time or in one sitting. Please feel free to attend to these tasks in your own time.

Considering the Shame Cluster

Box 1.9

Reflecting on Feelings of Shame

Shame Cluster (Feelings)

The Shame cluster includes experiences of feeling humiliated, embarrassed, inadequate, flawed, worthless, and similar feelings. Do you recognize any of such feelings in your own experience when you experienced difficult situations? If yes, please write them in the space provided. *(Use as much space as you need.)*

_____

_____

_____

_____

_____

_____

_____

_____

Box 1.10

Reflecting on Unmet Needs in Shame

Shame Cluster (Unmet Emotional Needs)

Now, as before, please try to reflect on the corresponding emotional needs (e.g., such as being accepted, valued, recognized, and so on) related to the Shame feeling. Please write them in the space provided. *(Use as much space as you need.)*

_____

_____

_____

_____

_____

_____

_____

Considering the Fear Cluster

Box 1.11

Reflecting on Feelings of Fear

Fear Cluster (Feelings)

The Fear cluster consists of experiences of being scared, unprotected, terrified, and such related feelings. If you can recognize some of these feelings that you may have experienced in a difficult situation in your own life, please write them here in the space provided. *(Use as much space as you need.)*

Box 1.12

Reflecting on Unmet Needs in Fear

Fear Cluster (Unmet Emotional Needs)

Now please try to write the corresponding emotional needs (such as being safe, protected, and so on) that relate to the Fear feelings. Please write them in the space provided. *(Use as much space as you need.)*

Task 3: Triggers of Emotional Pain

When we look closer at what triggers our emotional reactions, our research suggests that we can identify three main types of triggers. Each type is loosely related to one of the three clusters of emotional pain mentioned in the last section. Triggers such as loss or being excluded by significant people in our lives are associated with experiences from the sadness/loneliness cluster of emotional pain. Triggers of rejection or judgement usually tend to trigger feelings from the shame cluster of emotions. Situations of danger trigger feelings from the fear cluster of emotions. It is important to note that we often experience a mixture of different triggers. For instance, if we are rejected by a loved one, we may feel both alone and negatively judged, consequently feeling sadness and loneliness as well as shame.

Taking some time to become aware of your own emotional triggers can help you become aware of your personal vulnerabilities in terms of the different events and experiences that helped shape these over the course of your life. Being aware of such triggers can also help you become more aware of your responses to the emotions that these evoke (see Boxes 1.13, 1.14, and 1.15).

Note: Remember that you do not need to undertake all the following tasks at one time or in one sitting. Please feel free to attend to these tasks in your own time. You can always look up the completed examples from this chapter for Timothy and Alice in Appendix I (pages 133–157) if you need further guidance, clarification, or reference about how to undertake the task.

Box 1.13

Reflecting on Recent Triggers of Emotional Pain

Emotional Triggers (Recent)

Try to reflect on a *recent* emotionally charged situation in your life. What triggers did you encounter? *For example: loss, exclusion, rejection, danger.* Please write them in the space provided. *(Use as much space as you need.)*

_____

_____

_____

_____

_____

_____

_____

_____

_____

Box 1.14

Reflecting on Past Triggers of Emotional Pain

Emotional Triggers (Lifespan)

Now, please take a few moments to write down examples of the important triggers that you have felt shaped or affected by throughout the course of your life (e.g., loss, exclusion, rejection, danger). Such an exploration can often help in aiding us to become more aware of our personal emotional vulnerabilities. Please write them in the space provided. *(Use as much space as you need.)*

_____

_____

_____

_____

_____

_____

_____

_____

_____

_____

Box 1.15

Reflecting on Triggers of Emotional Pain and Corresponding Underlying Emotions

Triggers and Underlying Emotions (Lifespan)

Take a few moments to identify what underlying emotions (as opposed to symptoms of distress) were triggered by the experiences you reflected on in the last task. Often such emotions include variants of experiences of loss, sadness, shame, and fear. Please write them in the space provided. *(Use as much space as you need.)*

_____

_____

_____

_____

_____

_____

_____

_____

_____

Note: Remember that you do not need to undertake all the following tasks at one time or in one sitting. Please feel free to attend to these tasks in your own time. You can always look up the completed examples from this chapter for Timothy and Alice in Appendix I (pages 133–157) if you need further guidance, clarification, or reference about how to undertake the task.

Task 4: Emotional and Behavioural Avoidance

Experiencing painful feelings is unpleasant. That is why we have a tendency to avoid them or to dampen such feelings, if at all possible. This is known as 'emotional avoidance'. Sometimes we also avoid situations that could potentially bring about painful or unpleasant feelings. This is known as 'behavioural avoidance'.

Two forms of problematic self-relating (problematic self-treatment) also fulfil the function of assisting us in avoiding our emotions. Firstly, we could be excessively worrying ourselves (self-worry), as if we were almost preparing ourselves for potential scenarios that would stir up painful feelings in us – for instance, possible loss, exclusion, rejection, or danger. This causes us then to act on those worries by engaging in behavioural avoidance. For instance, a person worries that their public talk will not be well-received. This worrying will make them anxious that they will be judged to be a terrible presenter. Here, the person might be setting themselves up to prepare for the scenarios that could stir up feelings of humiliation and shame. Such worrying could lead them to either overprepare and/or avoid speaking at all. These are forms of behavioural avoidance and are intended to protect this person from feelings of shame. The worrying, however, has its own costs. It may not only lead us to avoid (or exhaust ourselves with overpreparation), but the worrying also serves to keep us feeling anxious. Paradoxically, anxiety may be more 'acceptable' to us, as it may be a more familiar feeling and a better trade-off for not feeling the even more upsetting feeling of humiliation and shame. We will look at the processes involved in worrying more closely in Chapter 4.

The other form of problematic self-treatment is 'self-interruption' (stopping oneself from feeling or expressing feelings), wherein we may attempt to stop or dampen any feelings or emotions before they can fully manifest themselves or we find ways to stop expressing our feelings at all. This may be done through various strategies, such as: distracting ourselves (focusing on other things), tightening up, or perhaps by numbing our sensations (e.g., using substances, or inflicting physical pain/deliberate self-harm to our bodies). It is important to note that we may not be fully aware that we are engaging in such self-interrupting behaviour. Sometimes we may express other emotions (for instance, anger), because it is easier to express that, than some underlying vulnerable emotion such as humiliation or shame. Or we may engage in other avoidant behaviours, such as leaving the situation completely. We will look at the processes involved in self-interrupting more closely in Chapter 3. The following tasks are designed to help you capture these two types of emotional avoidance (i.e., worrying and self-interrupting emotions) in yourself (see Boxes 1.16–1.21).

Note: Remember that you do not need to undertake all the following tasks at one time or in one sitting. Please feel free to attend to these tasks in your own time. You can always look up the completed examples from this chapter for Timothy and Alice in Appendix I (pages 133–157) if you need further guidance, clarification, or reference about how to undertake the task.

Considering Worrying

Box 1.16

Reflecting on Worrying

Enacting the Worrying

What are the situations you would typically worry about or were worried about recently (e.g., talking to your manager)? Please write them here in the space provided. *(Use as much space as you need.)*

_____

_____

_____

_____

_____

_____

_____

_____

_____

Box 1.17

Reflecting on the Impact of Worrying

Impact of Worrying

How does such worrying make you feel (e.g., anxious)? Please write in the space provided. *(Use as much space as you need.)*

_____

_____

_____

_____

_____

_____

_____

_____

Box 1.18

Reflecting on Worrying and Avoided Underlying Emotions

Avoided Underlying Emotions

When worrying about such situations, what are the emotions that you want to prevent yourself from feeling? What are the emotions that you were worried the situation would stir up in you (e.g., *"feeling ashamed if my line manager criticised me"*)? Please write here in the space provided the emotions that fit the situation you were worried about. *(Use as much space as you need.)*

_____

_____

_____

_____

_____

_____

_____

_____

Box 1.19

Reflecting on Worrying and Avoided Behaviour

Avoided Behaviour

Has your worrying also ever led you to avoid a situation? If yes, please write in the space provided about the situation(s) which you avoided, based on your earlier experience of worrying about it. *(Use as much space as you need.)*

_____

_____

_____

_____

_____

_____

_____

_____

Considering Self-Interruption

Box 1.20

Reflecting on Interruption of Emotions

Interruption of Emotions (Self-Interruption)

Can you reflect on a time when you stopped yourself from feeling a particular emotion (such as getting angry or feeling sad)? Please write about your experience(s) of self-interruption (stopping your emotions) here in the space provided. How did you stop yourself from feeling or expressing your emotions (e.g., deflecting from feeling, distracting yourself, tightening up, drinking alcohol)? *(Use as much space as you need.)*

_____

_____

_____

_____

_____

_____

_____

_____

_____

Box 1.21

Reflecting on the Impact of the Interruption of Emotions

Impact of Self-Interruption

What has been the impact of stopping/interrupting yourself from feeling things in your life? Please write about it here in the space provided. *(Use as much space as you need.)*

_____

_____

_____

_____

_____

_____

_____

_____

Task 5: Problematic Self-Relating (How We Treat Ourselves with Self-Criticism)

When we react to emotional triggers in our lives, it is important to notice that we tend to treat ourselves in particular ways. This is a very typical response as we try to adjust ourselves in the context of our interactions with others. For example, if our friend or partner is upset after an argument with us, it is normal for us to reflect on how we were in the argument (e.g., "*was I too hard on them?*"). On the other hand, we may also develop ways of relating to ourselves that are not particularly helpful. For instance, we may either judge ourselves for not fulfilling our goals (e.g., "*I wasn't able to explain where I was coming from without hurting them*") or judge ourselves for how we are in interactions with others (e.g., "*I acted stupidly; I am stupid*"). Self-criticism is an example of a problematic way of how we tend to treat ourselves in the context of difficult triggers. Therefore, not only do we feel the pain of being rejected by another person (or feel disappointed for not achieving our goal), but we may also worsen the situation by blaming ourselves for it. *This ends up making us feeling even more hurt.* Please look at the tasks that lead you on your ways of criticizing yourself (see Boxes 1.22–1.23).

Note: Remember that you do not need to undertake all the following tasks at one time or in one sitting. Please feel free to attend to these tasks in your own time. You can always look up the completed examples from this chapter for Timothy and Alice in Appendix I (pages 133–157) if you need further guidance, clarification, or reference about how to undertake the task.

Box 1.22

Reflecting on Own Self-Criticism

Criticizing the Self

Do you judge yourself? If so, how do you criticize yourself? Please write it here in the space provided. *(Use as much space as you need.)*

   Note: Try to focus on the manner of judgement of yourself as a person (*for instance, "I am a fool, I am too weak, I am not smart enough, I am inadequate, I am not looking good enough …"*).

_____

_____

_____

_____

_____

_____

_____

_____

The Role of Emotions in Our Lives 25

Box 1.23

Reflecting on the Impact of Self-Criticism

Noticing the Impact of Judgement

Now try to notice what happens inside you when you criticize yourself like this (often we tend to feel small, worthless, inadequate, flawed, unlovable, not good enough…). Please write here, in the space provided, any feelings (or physical sensations) that you notice as you criticize yourself (*e.g., "I feel unlovable"*). *(Use as much space as you need.)*

_____

_____

_____

_____

_____

_____

_____

_____

_____

_____

_____

_____

_____

Note: Remember that you do not need to undertake all the following tasks at one time or in one sitting. Please feel free to attend to these tasks in your own time.

Task 6: Interpersonal Emotional Injuries

Many triggers of emotional pain are of an interpersonal nature. We may have experienced long-lasting or particularly significant (emotionally salient) experiences of exclusion, loss, rejection, abuse, and threats in the past or we may have had such similar experiences in very recent times. These types of interpersonal experiences can often become pivotal in shaping our *emotional vulnerabilities*.

What is emotional vulnerability? Emotional vulnerability is sensitivity to situations or interactions that are similar in nature to pivotal *emotional injuries* we have experienced previously (e.g., often during developmentally significant periods in our lives).

We will focus more on these type of experiences in Chapter 6 where we look at the possibility of healing from emotional injuries. In this task, you will deepen your understanding about the impact of interpersonal emotional injuries by reflecting on specific examples from your own life. Here we will start to reflect on your emotional injuries (see Boxes 1.24 and 1.25).

Note: Remember that you do not need to undertake all the tasks at one time or in one sitting. Please feel free to attend to these tasks in your own time. You can always look up the completed examples from this chapter for Timothy and Alice in Appendix I (pages 133–157) if you need further guidance, clarification, or reference about how to undertake the task.

Considering Emotional Injuries

Box 1.24

Reflecting on Own Emotional Injuries

Emotional Injuries

Reflect on some past (or recent, ongoing) interpersonal situations (e.g., where a [significant] person in your life was critical of you, threatened you, disapproved of you, was unavailable, or did not have capacity [felt too vulnerable] to be with you) that brought emotional pain to you. You can start with an example that is not that painful. Please describe the situation, the behaviour of the other, and the message you received from such behaviour in the space provided. *(Use as much space as you need.)*

Box 1.25

Reflecting on the Impact of Emotional Injuries

Emotional Injuries (Checking for Pain)

Now check inside, do you experience any sense of lingering hurt from the situation you just described? What are the lingering feelings that you may have, that are connected to these painful situations and interactions? Please list them in the space provided. *(Use as much space as you need.)*

_____

_____

_____

_____

_____

_____

_____

_____

_____

_____

_____

_____

_____

Chapter Summary

Let us now recap on some of the key points that you have learned in this chapter:

1 You learned how to distinguish symptomatic distress (e.g., depression and anxiety) from specific underlying vulnerable emotions (e.g., sadness/loneliness, shame, fear) that point to unmet emotional needs (e.g., to be connected, to be valued, to be safe).

2 You learned that common triggers of emotional pain are interpersonal injuries (loss/being excluded by significant people; rejection/judgement) and situations of danger.

3 You also learned that problematic ways of trying to avoid emotions include self-worrying and self-interruption. These are forms of emotional avoidance that may lead to avoidant behaviour (e.g., avoiding situations that could bring painful emotions).

4 You explored that while many painful emotions are interpersonal in nature, some are also responses to a person's own self-treatment such as self-criticism.

5 You learned that emotional sensitivity (vulnerability) to specific situations and interactions is shaped by previous pivotal hurtful experiences.

Quiz for Self-Assessment (See Appendix I, page 158 for Answers)

	True	False
1 Emotions provide us with information about how well we are getting on in our relationships.	☐	☐
2 Depression is a form of Symptomatic Distress.	☐	☐
3 Anxiety is a possible symptom of emotional pain.	☐	☐
4 Love and Connection are antidotes to experiences of loneliness, chronic sadness, and loss.	☐	☐
5 Unmet emotional needs may include our need to feel connected, to feel valued, and to feel safe.	☐	☐
6 Self-Worrying is a problematic way of responding to emotions.	☐	☐

Chapter 2

Optimal Use of Emotions

Learning Goals

1 To learn to connect with and stay with your emotions even when they feel difficult.
2 To learn the 'Clearing a Space' task and the 'Compassionate Self-Soothing' task as the foundation for your subsequent experiential work and as a tool for regulating your emotions when they feel too intense.

Suggested duration: One week

Introduction

The transformation of chronic painful emotions is the key focus of our work in this workbook. However, before we are able to transform chronic painful emotions, we need to ensure that we first build our capacity to tolerate and be curious about our emotional experiences. At times we may feel overwhelmed by our emotions, while at other times we may feel completely disconnected from our emotions and therefore find ourselves being unable to focus on what these emotions are telling us.

This chapter will introduce tasks that can help you connect with and befriend your emotions. The Clearing a Space and Compassionate Self-Soothing tasks are particularly useful for times when you are feeling too upset and overwhelmed with your emotions and would like to regulate them. However, please remember that when you are practicing these tasks for the first few times, you may experience difficulties in using them to their full potential. It will be helpful to repeat these tasks several times to deepen their impact to help you with your emotional regulation. We will now discuss these tasks in more detail and then proceed to practicing them.

> Note: Remember that you do not need to undertake all the following tasks at one time or in one sitting. Please feel free to attend to these tasks in your own time. You can always look up the completed examples from this chapter for Timothy and Alice in Appendix II (pages 159–160) if you need further guidance, clarification, or reference about how to undertake the task.

DOI: 10.4324/9781003201861-3

The 'Clearing a Space' Task

The Clearing a Space[1] task is designed to help regulate overwhelming emotional experiences. You should only use this task when you are feeling a sense of being overwhelmed. The task first seeks to assist you in identifying where the distress is being felt in your body and then proceeds to guide you in naming that felt experience and gently putting it aside at a safe and comfortable distance. The process of identifying where we feel distress and then putting the upsetting feeling aside is repeated until you experience a sense of relief. The steps of the task are now discussed in more detail.

Description of Main Stages of the Clearing a Space Task

In this section we briefly explain the main steps that are involved in this task. This is helpful to prepare you for the task and provide the rationale behind it. Please note that you don't need to undertake these steps at this time. You will be provided with detailed guidance sheets in this chapter that are designed to be used when you are ready to undertake the task. Use this section only as an educational piece to help you become familiar with what to expect in the task and use the detailed guidance sheets when you are ready to practice the task.

When to use the task: Use any time when you are feeling upset or overwhelmed. If you are not currently feeling upset, but want to practice the task, you can always think about a mildly upsetting situation. Indeed, it is even better to practice with less upsetting feelings.

Number of stages: There are six main stages in the Clearing a Space task, as explained in the following:

Stage 1 – Direct your Attention Inwards

In Stage 1 you begin the task by directing your attention inwards, typically to the middle of your body (i.e., stomach and chest areas). This is the area where we tend to feel our emotions physically most strongly.

Stage 2 – Attempt to Describe the Bodily Feelings

This stage is about finding words to describe the bodily feelings related to the upsetting situation (or the upset you feel). See what words feel right to you.

Stage 3 – Give a Name to the Feeling

Now try to give a name to the feeling, labelling it in a way that captures both the internal experience and connects the feeling with the external situation that may have triggered it. For example, in this step you may notice something like "*a weight in my chest like there is a lead bucket placed on it* that has *to do with my upcoming exam*".

Stage 4 – Imagine Putting the Feeling Aside

Imagine putting this feeling that you described and labelled aside and away from yourself temporarily. For example, you may imagine that you are putting "*the lead bucket beside you on the floor*".

Stage 5 – Direct Your Attention Inwards Once Again

In Stage 5, after imagining yourself putting that labelled feeling aside, you can again focus inwards and try to see what it is that you can sense now that, for instance, the weighing feeling has been cleared aside (after this bucket of lead was put aside).

Stage 6 – Repeat Stages 1 to 5 until you Experience a Sense of Relief

At this point your feeling may change or a new feeling linked to the same or a different situation may arise (e.g., I feel that the bucket is not so close to me now and I do not feel such a weight, but still feel a bit of tension). Again, repeat Stages 1 to 5, describing and labelling the feeling (trying to give it a shape [e.g., ball, bucket, stone] so it would be easier to put it aside later) and if possible, also the situation that it is linked to (e.g., a bit of tension that is linked to the fact that I did not study as much as I wanted). Then, once again, put it aside in your imagination. Repeat the process until you feel a sense of relief within your body.

Note: It is likely that it will take some time and practice with the task before you are fully successful in reaching this sense of relief – that is normal and to be expected. However, it is important to allow yourself to appreciate any signs of any change, even if they seem subtle.

Some people find the idea of putting such internal experiences of tension or discomfort aside, even in an imaginary way, difficult. This is often because they are fearful that they will forget something or that they may leave themselves open to new and less familiar sensations. It is important to remember that this is just a temporary measure, and it will not mean that you will forget to go about your business as required or that you will spend a long time connecting with a new or uncomfortable experience. If you were getting anxious when you put a feeling aside, try not to put it too far away (e.g., just beside you on the floor or on a table in your room). It may signal that the feeling reminds you of a situation you want to attend to and you are getting anxious that it is now outside your control. So put it aside but not too far and remember you can reach out to it anytime you need it. You are putting the feelings aside only temporarily. They are likely to come back spontaneously as your mind engages with the difficult situation that triggers them.

Hopefully, this will all make a lot more sense when you practice the task using the guidance sheet in the next section. You do not need to worry about remembering all the steps, as the guidance sheets will give you clear instructions about what to do at every stage of the task. Remember, you can use the guidance sheets provided in this book or you can download a copy of the guidance sheets from the accompanying Support Material (www.routledge.com/9781032063393), print them out and use them independently for easy and quick reference. You can also review how Timothy and Alice worked through this task in Boxes 2.2 and 2.3.

Clearing a Space Guidance Sheets

STAGE I

DIRECT YOUR ATTENTION INWARDS

--

1 This task is suitable when you are upset. The upset may be related to a specific situation or issue, or it may be unclear.
2 Please be seated in a comfortable position. You can also close your eyes if you are comfortable to do so.
3 Begin to pay attention to the middle part of your body. This is often the region where we feel most of our upsetting feelings.
4 Take a moment to observe this within yourself.
5 When you are ready, move on to Stage 2.

STAGE 2

ATTEMPT TO DESCRIBE THE BODILY FEELING

--

1   When you notice any unpleasant or intense feeling, try to describe it.
2   Describe the feeling for yourself and make a note about what in your life the feeling may be referring to.
3   When you are ready, move on to Stage 3.

STAGE 3

GIVE A NAME TO THE FEELING

--

1 You can now try to name the feeling that you have described to yourself (i.e., try and label it).
2 Try also to name the situation or the issue the feeling relates to.
3 Note: It is desirable that the labelling also references the experience in your body as well as the situation that brings that feeling. For instance, *"I feel butterflies in my stomach (bodily feeling)"* and *"it is related to my upcoming meeting with my boss"* (situation). See what label (name) fits right for the unpleasant feeling that you are experiencing.
4 See what labels feel right for you.
5 When you are ready, move on to Stage 4.

STAGE 4

IMAGINE PUTTING THE FEELING ASIDE

--

1 Now, imagine putting this labelled feeling at some distance from yourself. For instance, in the corner of the room or outside the room.
2 You can choose any place that feels right to put it to.
3 You can also imagine it going (being put) into a box.
4 When you are ready, move on to Stage 5.

STAGE 5

DIRECT YOUR ATTENTION INWARDS ONCE AGAIN

--

1 Once you have set the unpleasant feeling aside, pay attention once again to the middle of your body, and see how you are feeling now.
2 Are you (a) more upset or do you (b) sense some relief?
3 If you are (a) more upset, it usually means that the upset was linked to something you want to keep on your mind and putting it aside made you more anxious. In that case try to put the upsetting feeling not far away so you could have it within a reach if you needed it.
4 If you feel (b) any relief, enjoy it.
5 When you are ready, move on to Stage 6.

STAGE 6

REPEAT STAGES I TO 5 UNTIL YOU EXPERIENCE RELIEF

--

1 As you continue to pay attention to the middle part of your body, see whether there are any other unpleasant feelings still present.
2 If there are, please repeat the process from the beginning at Stage 1.
3 Continue with the process for as many times as needed until you have a sense that you put at least some of the unpleasant feelings aside. Sometimes we are reluctant to put some of the feelings aside, particularly those worries that we think are preparing us for important situations in our lives. In that case, please try to remember that you are putting them aside just for a moment, and you will be able to attend to them whenever you need to.

Note: The Clearing a Space task can be used alongside all the other experiential tasks in this workbook, so please feel free to return to this foundational task to help you regulate any overwhelming emotions at any time.

Clearing a Space – Summary

Well-done on completing the Clearing a Space task. If you experienced some relief, you have just cleared some space within. You may now want to repeat the task to deepen this sense of relief. Alternatively, if you did not experience any degree of relief and are still feeling a bit overwhelmed it might be useful to re-attempt this task. Remember, you can return to this task at any time you feel the need to regulate an overwhelming emotional experience. You can now proceed to Box 2.1 and write a few summary notes about your experience of this exercise. This can be useful for consolidating your learning.

Box 2.1

Clearing a Space (Summary of Experience)

Clearing a Space (Summary of Experience)

Use this space to write down a few summary notes about your experience of the 'Clearing a Space' task and how you felt after completing the same. You can compare your notes with those of Timothy and Alice provided in Boxes 2.2 and 2.3.

_____

_____

_____

_____

_____

_____

_____

_____

_____

_____

_____

Box 2.2

Clearing a Space (Summary of Experience: Timothy)

What Timothy was doing during the Clearing a Space task

I tried this clearing a space task after seeing one of Rachel's posts on social media. I noticed myself feeling hot and panicky, my heart was racing, and my stomach was almost cramping up with discomfort, like there was a lead balloon in there pressing down on all my organs. She looked so happy surrounded by some of our friends and some new faces I didn't recognize. I think I was initially feeling exhilarated to see her and relieved she wasn't miserable but that was quickly replaced by a fear of what I was missing out on, who she might be spending her night with and what she was saying about me to others. I took a deep breath in and tried to use that breath to wrap around that fear/dread feeling in the pit of my stomach. I imagined breathing out that fear from my stomach into a glass jar I have sitting on the desk in my room. With each breath I tried to expel more of that weight and that fear. After five or six breaths I started noticing that I felt a bit lighter, but I became more aware of a pressure on my chest and around my heart. This felt more related to a sense of sadness and loss that I wasn't there with her, that I wouldn't be there with her again. It felt harder to put that pressure aside but after a few more breaths I imagined breathing the pressure out of my chest into an empty shoe box I had lying under the bed I started to feel calmer at least.

Box 2.3

Clearing a Space (Summary of Experience: Alice)

What Alice was doing during the Clearing a Space task

After an argument with my husband, I sat down on the sofa in my room and decided to try out the 'Clearing a Space' task. I took three slow and long breaths and started to pay attention to the sensations I felt around my chest. I noticed this sharp pain near my heart. It's like someone had just cut out a hole in my heart. It's like the words 'I am suffocating' just sliced right through my heart. I continued to take deep and long breaths and imagined putting this sharp pain in a bucket of ice on the table next to me. Next, I focused inwards again, the sharp pain was less intense, but I noticed some tightness around my throat. It's like someone was trying to strangulate me and words were being stuck in my throat and they couldn't come out. It's a feeling of being wronged by my husband and not understood by him. I took a couple of deep breaths and imagined putting these feelings of strangulation in the bucket of ice. After putting that feeling aside, I gently focused inwards again and felt more spacious and freed inside.

Quiz for Self-Assessment (See Appendix II, page 161 for Answers)

		True	False
1	Clearing a Space task should be used when you are feeling overwhelmed.	☐	☐
2	There are four stages involved in the Clearing a Space task.	☐	☐
3	Stage 1 of the Clearing a Space task requires you to pay attention to the middle part of the body.	☐	☐
4	Stage 2 of the Clearing a Space task requires you to imagine the uncomfortable feeling disappearing from your body.	☐	☐
5	Sometimes there might be a reluctance to put some of the feelings aside. This is because the feelings need to be put aside permanently.	☐	☐
6	The Clearing a Space task should be repeated as many times as required to deepen the sense of relief.	☐	☐

Note: The next section explores the Self-Soothing task. Remember that you do not need to undertake all the tasks at one time or in one sitting. Please feel free to attend to these tasks in your own time. You can always look up the completed examples from this chapter for Timothy and Alice in Appendix II (pages 159–160) if you need further guidance, clarification, or reference about how to undertake the task.

The 'Compassionate Self-Soothing' Task

The Compassionate Self-Soothing task has been developed to help regulate distress. Like the Clearing a Space task, this task too can be practiced when you are overwhelmed and upset. This task can also be practiced at the end of any other task if you are feeling distressed. In short, this task can be most effective in regulating any distressful feelings and is always available to you. This task is also different from the 'Clearing a Space' task. For this task you will need two chairs facing each other, i.e., your own chair and an empty chair opposite to your chair. See Figure 2.1 for clarity around how and where to position the chairs.

Pre-Exercise Requirements: For this task, you will need an empty chair placed opposite to your own chair. That is, the two chairs should be facing each other. The chair on the left will be the 'Self-Chair' for yourself, and the chair on the right will be for the imagined 'Compassionate-Other'. Please begin by being seated in a comfortable position in the 'Self-Chair' on the left and begin by focusing on your breathing. Throughout this task, remember to primarily focus on your feelings and emotions, rather than on your thoughts. Again, see Figure 2.1 for reference.

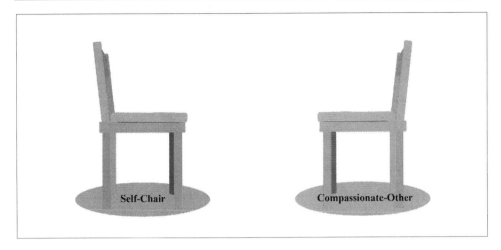

Figure 2.1 Chair positions for the Compassionate Self-Soothing task. Self-Chair is on the left side and the Compassionate-Other-Chair is on the right side.

Description of Main Stages of the 'Compassionate Self-Soothing' Task

In this section we briefly explain the main steps that are involved in this task. This is helpful to prepare you for the task and provide the rationale behind it. Please note that you don't need to undertake these steps at this time. You will be provided with detailed guidance sheets in this chapter that are designed to be used when you are ready to undertake the task. Use this section only as an educational piece to help you become familiar with what to expect in the task and use the detailed guidance sheets when you are ready to practice the task.

When to use the task: This task can be done at any time and may also be practiced any time outside the course, when you are feeling overwhelmed and want to bring in a sense of calm.

Number of stages: There are five main stages in the Compassionate Self-Soothing task, as explained in the following:

Stage 1 – Imagining the Other

In this stage you will be asked to sit on your chair (i.e., the Self-Chair) and think about a caring/compassionate 'Other' person. This basically means to think about any person in your life (or a fictional character) with whom you would feel comfortable sharing your distress and who has a calming effect on you.

Stage 2 – Expressing to the Other

Once you have decided who this person is, you can imagine this person sitting on the opposite chair and you can then express how you feel (your distress) to them.

Stage 3 – Being the Compassionate Other

In this next step, you are asked to swap the chair (you will be required to move yourself from the Self-Chair to the 'Other' chair opposite to you) and enact this other person. You are then asked to try to embody this caring/compassionate Other person. As this other person, you are then asked to convey and express their response to how you (in the Self-Chair, your original chair) feel right-here-right-now. Try to see whether you can convey this calming presence this person (usually) has on you. Let us say, for example, that you have chosen your grandmother to be your caring 'Other' person. Therefore, you will now be imagining yourself to be your grandmother and consider what she would be saying to you (how she would be with you) if she witnessed you, sitting in the Self-Chair in front of her, so distressed.

Stage 4 – Expressing as the Other

Now you will be asked to voice out loud all the caring feelings that the Other (i.e., in this case, the grandmother) feels towards you. Please try and embody your grandmother's pace and tone of expression, the kind of language she would use and what she would say.

Stage 5 – Letting the Compassion In

Finally, you are asked to return to the original 'Self' chair and experience how it feels for you to hear those caring words from the Other person (e.g., your grandmother) and being calmed by her.

Hopefully, this will all make a lot more sense when you practice the task using the guidance sheet on the next page. You do not need to worry about remembering all the steps, as the guidance sheets give you clear instructions at every stage.

Support Material: Remember, you can use the guidance sheets provided in this book or you can download a copy of the guidance sheets from the accompanying Support Material (www.routledge.com/9781032063393), print them out, and use them independently for easy and quick reference.

Compassionate Self-Soothing Task Guidance Sheets

STAGE 1

IMAGINING THE OTHER
(Seating Position: on the <u>Self-Chair</u> to the left)

--

1   Begin by thinking of a compassionate or caring person who you would feel comfortable sharing your distressing feelings with.
2   Once you have thought of this person, look at the empty chair in front of you and imagine that the compassionate Other that you have selected is sitting on that chair.
3   Try to imagine what the person looks like, their facial expressions, and how they are looking at you too.
4   When you have done so, please proceed to Stage 2.

Note: Remember that this compassionate Other person can be anyone, from any time. For instance, it could be a (former) friend, partner, parent, sibling, teacher, grandparent (who may be now deceased), or a spiritual being. It does not have to be a person who is available to you in everyday life, they can be from the past too.

STAGE 2

EXPRESSING TO THE OTHER
(Seating Position: on the <u>Self-Chair</u> to the left)

--

1 Now tell the caring Other (in the Compassionate-Other-Chair) what emotionally distresses you. Use as much detail as possible in describing your distress.
2 Take as much time as you need.
3 When you have finished expressing to the caring Other person what distresses you, please get up from Self-Chair and sit on the Compassionate-Other-Chair on the right).
4 Now please proceed to Stage 3.

STAGE 3

BEING THE COMPASSIONATE OTHER
(Seating Position: on the <u>Compassionate-Other-Chair</u> on the right)

--

1 Now imagine being this caring/compassionate Other.
2 Try to see how he or she feels towards you. How would this person feel when they see you so distressed? What would they wish for you? What would they be able to offer you to help you feel better?
3 When you have done so, please proceed to Stage 4.

STAGE 4

EXPRESSING AS THE COMPASSIONATE OTHER
(Seating Position: on the <u>Compassionate-Other-Chair</u> on the right)

--

1 Take a moment to express to yourself what this Compassionate-Other person is expressing, at this time when you feel so distressed.
2 Enact this person's caring words, or voice them out loud as if speaking to yourself in the Self-Chair.
3 Continue to sit on the caring/compassionate person's chair and express what this caring person would wish to tell you. How would they be with you? How would they try to calm you?
4 Please take as much time as you need to do this step.
5 When you have fully expressed as the caring Other, please move to the Self-Chair.
6 Now please proceed to Stage 5.

STAGE 5

LETTING THE COMPASSION IN
(Seating Position: on the <u>Self-Chair</u> to the left)

--

1 Now, back in the Self-Chair, please take a moment to see how it feels for you to get such caring words from this compassionate person.
2 What is the sense inside? Stay with it and voice it aloud.
3 Express how you are feeling now to this imagined Compassionate-Other person. Tell them how it felt to get that care from them.
4 Take as much time as you need to complete this final step.
5 Well-done. You have now completed this task.

Compassionate Self-Soothing – Summary

Well-done on completing the 'Compassionate Self-Soothing' task. Hopefully, in doing this task, you experienced some sense of relief from distressful feelings. At this stage it might be beneficial to repeat this task, if you feel like it, and deepen this sense of relief and caring for yourself. Alternatively, you can also consider attempting the previous task, '*Clearing a Space*', to regulate any distress that you may be experiencing. Once you are ready, please review the narrative examples of Timothy and Alice in Boxes 2.4 and 2.5, as they recount their own experiences of completing the Compassionate Self-Soothing task. When you have reviewed the same, you can then proceed to complete the summary sheet provided in this section (Box 2.6) to record your own experience of this experiential task.

Box 2.4

Compassionate Self-Soothing (Summary of Experience: Timothy)

What Timothy was doing during the Compassionate Self-Soothing task

I thought of my best friend from the gym. We've only known each other a couple of years now but I remember when I first met him it felt like he really got me, like he was the brother I never had. I can be open with him about how much I'm doubting myself, how I'm worrying about every little detail in work and how I'm convincing myself I'll get fired. He sat in the Compassionate-Other-Chair looking relaxed and curious, dressed in a tracksuit for work. I then swapped the chair and enacted him. He (me as him) was concerned about me, and he seemed sad to see me feeling so distressed. He asked me "what's happened to make you think that?", "what can I do to help?". He said, "I understand what you're going through, I've been there too" and he reassured me "you are overthinking it; you'd got a lot to offer, people really respect you around here". He told me that I'm fine, and that everything would get better. He suggested we get a training session in together and go for something to eat. When I returned to the Self-Chair I felt a lot lighter and like I could breathe deeply again. I was so grateful to him for just being there and for being able to understand what I'm going through. I was relieved he understood, and he still wanted to hang out.

Box 2.5

Compassionate Self-Soothing (Summary of Experience: Alice)

What Alice was doing during the Compassionate Self-Soothing task

I thought of my deceased maternal grandmother. She looked concerned and her gaze was gentle and soft. As I enacted her in the Compassionate-Other-Chair, she (me as her) felt a lot of love for me. She was sad to see me feel so hurt. She wished for me to be happy, and she offered to cook my favourite corn soup to comfort me. She said to me that I was very precious to her, and that she loves me just the way I am. She knows that I get angry because I love others very deeply. When I returned to the Self-Chair, my heart felt warm, and it felt like a heavy weight had been lifted. Thank you, Grandma, for getting me and I feel understood and accepted by you.

Box 2.6

Summary Sheet: Compassionate Self-Soothing Task

Parts Enacted in the Self-Chair	Parts Enacted in the Compassionate-Other-Chair
This is what I feel when I am distressed:	
	This is how the caring/compassionate person that would understand my distress would be with me:
	This is how I felt towards myself when I enacted that caring Other person:
This is how it felt to receive their caring presence:	

Note: You can find the filled examples of Timothy and Alice's versions of the Summary Sheet in Appendix II (pages 159–160).

Quiz for Self-Assessment (See Appendix II, page 161 for Answers)

		True	False
1	The Compassionate Self-Soothing task should be used when you want to focus on your level of emotional vulnerability.	☐	☐
2	The Compassionate Self-Soothing task has been designed to help you in regulating distress.	☐	☐
3	Unlike the Clearing a Space task, the Compassionate Self-Soothing task should not be practiced when you are feeling upset.	☐	☐
4	The Compassionate Self-Soothing task can be used at any time you are feeling distressed and want to experience some relief.	☐	☐

Note

1 The Clearing a Space task stems from the work of Eugene Gendlin (1996) and is further inspired by the formulation of Robert Elliott et al. (2004).

Chapter 3

Overcoming Emotional Avoidance (The Self-Interrupter)

Learning Goals

1 To build on the previous chapter and become more aware about how we can sometimes become emotionally avoidant.
2 To learn an experiential task focused on emotional interruption (i.e., also known as self-interruption).
3 To use the experiential task to be able to feel and express important emotional experiences, rather than interrupt them, so those experiences could better inform your actions and behaviours.

Suggested duration: One week

Introduction

The main goal of this course is to work on the transformation of underlying painful emotions. However, at times emotions may be difficult to bear and therefore we may instead want to avoid them as much as we can. There are several ways in which we can avoid our feelings or bypass expressing our emotions. These can include strategies such as self-distracting, keeping oneself busy, worrying too much about the future, using substances such as alcohol to regulate or supress our feelings, engaging in behavioural avoidance to avoid or entirely leave certain situations that would stir up difficult emotions, and so on. In this chapter we will focus particularly on the strategy of interrupting our emotions and in the next chapter we will look at worrying. Interruption of emotions (we also refer to it as **Self-Interruption**[1]) is when we stop ourselves from feeling or from expressing feelings. The following task is designed to help you learn how to transform the Self-Interruption of emotions. This task will be particularly useful to undertake when you are feeling afraid of expressing some of your feelings or when you catch yourself wanting to avoid feelings. In this task, therefore, you will real-play and bring into contact two opposing parts of yourself, the Self and the Inner Self-Interrupter part. Both these opposing parts will sit on different chairs.

   Pre-Task Requirements: For this task, you will need two chairs: your own chair and an empty chair placed opposite your own chair. That is, the two chairs should be facing each other. The chair on the left will be called the **Experiencer-Chair**, and the chair on the right will be called the **Interrupter-Chair**. See Figure 3.1 for reference. Please be seated in the Experiencer-Chair at the start of the task in a comfortable position and begin by focusing on your breathing.

DOI: 10.4324/9781003201861-4

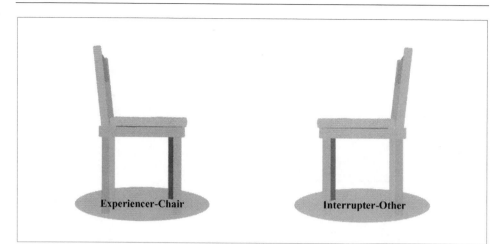

Figure 3.1 Chair positions for the Overcoming Self-Interruption task. Experiencer-Chair is on the left side and Interrupter-Chair is on the right side.

Description of Main Stages of the 'Overcoming the Self-Interrupter' Task

In this section we briefly explain the main steps that are involved in this task. This is helpful to prepare you for the task and provide the rationale behind it. Please note that you don't need to undertake these instructions at this time. You will be provided with detailed guidance sheets in this chapter that are designed to be used when you are ready to undertake the task. Use this section only as an educational piece to help you become familiar with what to expect in the task and use the detailed guidance sheets when you are ready to practice the task.

When to use the task: Normally you will use this task only at the moment when you catch yourself not wanting to feel something. You may try it out at first by remembering a situation (an issue) that brought feelings you did not want to feel. Throughout this task, remember to focus on your feelings and emotions, rather than on your thoughts. Remember also to take as much time as you need to complete the stages.

Number of stages: There are six main stages in the Overcoming the Self-Interrupter task, as explained here:

Stage 1 – Becoming Aware of the Interruption

Be seated in the Experiencer-Chair on the left side. Normally you will use this task only at the moment when you catch yourself not wanting to feel something. You can also try practicing this task out by remembering a situation that brought about feelings you did not want to feel. Start by taking a moment to reflect on the emotionally important issue or situation that brings in feelings that you do not want to feel or that you would be afraid of expressing (e.g., to the person they are related to).

Stage 2 – Enactment of Interruption

In this stage, you are guided to move to the Interrupter-Chair on the right. First, you are asked to consider the ways in which you stop yourself from feeling (i.e., think about how you block yourself or interrupt your expression of the feelings). Then you are asked to try to enact that part of yourself that interrupts you and stops you from feeling or prevents you from expressing your feelings. Here you are guided to consider how you (now as the Interrupter) stop the Self from feeling or from expressing these feelings. Express this out loud towards the Experiencer-Chair. This may be happening through giving yourself messages (e.g., *that feeling is too painful so just don't go there* or *don't say anything, if you do you're just going to hurt the other person involved or the other person involved won't be able to hear you or won't do anything about it*), or physically stopping oneself from feeling (e.g., by tightening muscles, grinding teeth, clenching fists, numbing self) or stopping oneself from activities that could bring pain (e.g., don't talk to others, they would laugh at you). Try to enact those interrupting actions (messages) as if you were doing them to somebody else. Imagine you are doing it to yourself sitting in the Experiencer-Chair. Make sure that the Self imagined in the Experiencer-Chair is constricted or blocked from his or her feelings.

Stage 3 – Impact of the Interruption

In Stage 3, after you have clearly enacted the Interrupter part of you, you will be asked to return to the Experiencer-Chair, and to become the Self again. Here you will be guided to check inwards on how such interruption of your feelings affects your internal experience and how it makes you feel (e.g., feeling constricted, blocked, tense, missing out, etc.). Then you will be guided towards expressing these feelings to the Interrupter on the other chair (e.g., *I feel constricted by you, blocked, tense, as if I was missing out, etc.*).

Stage 4 – Expressing the Need for Freer Expression

Now when you feel the impact of the Interrupter, try to articulate what you need from the Interrupter (e.g., *I need you to stop limiting me/shutting me down/silencing me*). You will then be asked to express what it is that you need from the interrupter.

Stage 5 – Probing for Compassion from the Interrupter

The next stage starts once you have clearly expressed what you need from the Interrupter. You will be guided to come back to the Interrupter-Chair and once again be the Interrupter part. The Interrupter part will be guided here to express to the Self part in the Experiencer-Chair how it is to hear the Self part speak about the negative impact of all the interruption and what the Interrupter feels towards the Experiencer. Here three things can happen:

1 The Interrupter panics and feels that it is too dangerous to let the Experiencer feel, express, or pursue behaviours that can bring up feelings and the Interrupter thus wants to ensure that constriction continues: In this case you will be guided to continue the task with Stage 5(A). **OR**
2 The Interrupter sees the impact of constriction and feels for the Experiencer and would want to stop interrupting but does not know how to as it is their automatic response: In this case you will also be guided to continue the task with Stage 5(A). **OR**

3   The Interrupter sees the impact of constriction and feels for the Experiencer and wants to try to let go of the interrupting: In this case you will be guided to continue the task with Stage 5(B).

Note: When you reach this point in the task, it is important to select the most appropriate pathway to continue on with. Stage 5(A) will help you when the interrupter is still unwilling to let go or wants to let go but doesn't know how to do so. Alternatively, Stage 5(B) will help you when the Interrupter is willing to cooperate with the Self and is willing to let go of the interruption.

Stage 6 – Building Effective Boundaries

Based on your experience in Stage 5, you will be required to complete either Stage 6(A) or Stage 6(B). If previously the Interrupter didn't soften or let go, now in Stage 6(A) you will be asked to sit in the Experiencer-Chair and see whether you can set a boundary with the relentless Interrupter (e.g. *Will you let him/her constrict you?*). Alternatively, if the Interrupter did soften, tried to let go, and expressed concern for the Self, now in Stage 6(B), you will be asked to sit in the Experiencer-Chair and let in the experience of this softening and see how it feels inside to get it.

As before, this should make a lot more sense when you practice the task using the guidance sheet on the next page. Remember, you do not need to worry about remembering all the steps, as the guidance sheets ahead give you clear instructions for every stage. You can also download copies of the guidance sheets from the accompanying Support Material (www.routledge.com/9781032063393), print them out, and use for easy and quick reference. You can also read through how Timothy and Alice approached this task in Boxes 3.1 and 3.2.

Overcoming the Self-Interrupter Guidance Sheets

STAGE I

BECOMING AWARE OF THE INTERRUPTION
(Seating Position: on the <u>Experiencer-Chair</u> to the left)

--

1 Please begin by being seated comfortably on the Experiencer-Chair.
2 You can use this task when you become aware that you are trying not to feel something that is upsetting, or when you are trying to avoid expressing some feelings, or when you are trying to avoid situations that could bring unpleasant feelings.
3 Alternatively, you can think about an emotionally important situation or issue that evokes feelings that you do not want to feel or that you would be afraid to express.
4 Consider the situation you would like to work on at this time.
5 Take as much time as you need.
6 When you are ready, please proceed to Stage 2.

STAGE 2

ENACTMENT OF INTERRUPTION
(Seating Position: on the <u>Interrupter-Chair</u> on the right)

--

1   Please move to the Interrupter-Chair on the right and try to enact that part of yourself that interrupts and stops your feelings.
2   What are the ways in which you stop yourself from such feelings? Reflect on how you block yourself, or interrupt the feelings, or the expression of the feelings of the Self?
3   Continue to think about how you ensure that the Self on the Experiencer-Chair does not feel, express, or be in situations where they may feel uncomfortable feelings?
4   Visualize yourself in the Experiencer-Chair and <u>say out loud or enact exactly</u> how you interrupt and block their feelings. Sometimes this is through verbal messages. Other times it can be through tightening up or constraining the Self in other ways.
5   Try to enact those interrupting actions (messages) as if you were doing them to somebody else. Imagine you are doing it to yourself sitting in the Experiencer-Chair.
6   Make sure that the Self imagined in the Experiencer-Chair is constricted. How do you do it?
7   Take as much time as you need to complete this stage.
8   When you are ready, please proceed to Stage 3.

STAGE 3

IMPACT OF THE INTERRUPTION
(Seating Position: on the <u>Experiencer-Chair</u> to the left)

--

1   When you have a sense that you have clearly enacted the Interrupter part of you, please return to the Experiencer-Chair.
2   How is it to be constricted by the Interrupter? How does it feel inside?
3   Now, try to feel how such blocking of your feelings or their expression affects your internal experience. How does it feel inside? What is your sense when you get this from the Interrupter? Take a breath and see how it feels for you. What happens inside when you are blocked like this?
4   Take a moment to tell the Interrupter on the other chair how it is for you when you are being blocked, interrupted. You may have experienced a whole range of different sensations when being obstructed. Tell the Interrupter what it is like for you to be blocked, interrupted, and obstructed.
5   Even though some of the interruption may have felt like it was warranted and was protecting you, try to stay with the sensations that the interruption and obstruction evoke in you. It is quite likely that it must be unpleasant to be interrupted from expressing your feelings and having your feelings blocked in this manner.
6   Try to notice any physical sensations that may be happening within your body. Can you voice out the feelings from that part of your body where such blocking impacts you most? People often feel that such interruptions bring tension, muscle-aches, tightening, or even a headache. Does any of this happen to you?
7   It is important that you tell the Interrupter part just how it feels inside. So, tell the Interrupter part how you are impacted.
8   Please take as much time as you need for expressing your experience to the Interrupter.
9   When you are ready, proceed to Stage 4.

STAGE 4

EXPRESSING THE NEED FOR FREER EXPRESSION
(Seating Position: on the <u>Experiencer-Chair</u> to the left)

--

1   Now, also tell the Interrupter, what you need from them as you feel all this inside. What do you need them to do? For instance, this could be something like "I need you to allow me to express my feelings" or "I want you to stop blocking my feelings".
2   Try to voice out what you really feel you need from the Interrupter part.
3   Remember to take as much time as you need to complete this stage.
4   When you feel that you have clearly voiced out what you really need from the Interrupter part, please move on to Stage 5.

STAGE 5

PROBING FOR COMPASSION FROM THE INTERRUPTER
(Seating Position: on the <u>Interrupter-Chair</u> to the right)

--

1 Once you have clearly expressed what you need from the Interrupter, please come back to the Interrupter-Chair.
2 Now as the Interrupter part, what do you feel towards the Experiencer? Towards this Self that feels so blocked or interrupted? What do you feel towards them? And what do you wish for them? Tell them how you feel towards them.
3 Now see whether you feel more like obstructing, protecting, interrupting yourself or do you now feel like letting go of your obstructing?
4 At this stage, consider whether you in the Interrupter-Chair want to continue interrupting (protecting the experiencer) or are willing to let go of interrupting. Sometimes it is a mixture of the two. Based on how you are feeling, choose <u>one</u> of the following options:

Choose one of the most appropriate options from 5(A) or 5(B).

5(A) Wanting to Continue Interrupting Further or Mixture of Feelings
1 If that is the case, try to identify what makes it difficult to let go of your inter-rupting. Usually this happens because we want to protect ourselves from painful feelings or possible negative consequences of emotional expression. Try to see the reasons behind your interrupting.
2 Express these to the experiencer: *I can't let go of interrupting/stopping your feelings as I am afraid that … .*
3 Say also that you will keep interrupting the Self: *I will keep stopping you from feel-ing, from expressing, from getting to the situations that could bring painful feelings because … .*
4 Now please move to the Experiencer-Chair and continue the task with Stage 6(A).

-Go now to Stage 6(A)-

5(B) Wanting to Let Go of the Interruption
1 As the Interrupter, you may see the impact of constriction and feel for the Self on the Experiencer-Chair, and you may feel like letting go of the interrupting.
2 Please take some time to express this feeling of wanting to let go of (over)protecting and stopping the Self in the Experiencer-Chair from feeling or expressing feelings.
3 Now please come back the Experiencer-Chair and continue with 'Stage 6(B)'

-Go now to Stage 6(B)-

STAGE 6(A)

BUILDING EFFECTIVE BOUNDARIES
(Seating Position: on the <u>Experiencer-Chair</u> to the left)

--

Remember: Use this Stage 6(A) if you (earlier as the Interrupter) had felt unwilling of letting go of interrupting or it is a mixture of letting go and interrupting at the same time.

1 It may be difficult to be further constricted, subject to so much restriction. What do you need in the face of all that restriction? What do you really need? Express it. It may be difficult to stand up for yourself, but if you were able to do that, what would you really need? For example, you might need to *"just be able to express my feelings"* or *"stop being held back"* or *"feel freer"*, and so on. Now tell the Interrupter what you really need and what you would do if you had the power to face the Interrupter. If you feel that power now say to the Interrupter that you feel it.
2 How does it feel when you say that? What was it like to stand up for yourself for what you need?
3 Now tell the Interrupter part how you felt when you stood up for yourself.
4 What will be your response to the Interrupter part if it keeps doing the blocking? Tell the Interrupter part what your response would be.
5 Now, take a moment to pause and reflect on how you feel inside now that you have been able to express yourself more freely than before. See how it feels inside to have been able to express yourself and take a few deep breaths.
6 Well-done. You have now completed the task.

STAGE 6(B)

LETTING IN SOFTENING
(Seating Position: on the <u>Experiencer-Chair</u> to the left)

--

Remember: Use the Stage 6(B) if you (earlier as the Interrupter) had felt like letting go of the interruption and are willing to stop interrupting.

1   So, there seems to be some softening coming from the Interrupter towards you. How is it to hear those softer words? Can you try to let some of it in? How does it feel inside?

2   There has been a lot of blocking of your feelings, and it might be difficult to take all this in. But just for a moment, could you check inside and see how it feels to be told from that Interrupter part that the Interrupter feels more understanding and caring towards you. Can you allow these feelings to come in?

3   Now, tell the Interrupter part how it feels for you inside. Tell them how it was to have received those softer words from them. Try to identify the feelings that were blocked previously and express them for yourself out loud. If they are directed to some person, imagine them and say it to them (as they come in your imagination) in the here and now.

4   Take a moment to pause and reflect on how you feel inside now that you have been able to express yourself more freely than before. See how it feels inside and take a few deep breaths.

5   Well-done. You have now completed the task.

Overcoming Self-Interruption – Summary

Well-done on completing the Overcoming Self-Interruption task. As we learnt, the self-interrupter prevents us from feelings that could be too painful and also leads to missing out on the important information they contain. Self-interruption often leaves us with uncomfortable physical sensations such as tension headaches, muscle-aches, and a sense of constriction in our chest. Hopefully, through attempting this task, you have become more aware of how you may be stopping your feelings and their expression and have started to understand the impact this has on you and on your life. This may have left you feeling motivated to try alternative ways of being with your feelings. If you are feeling any kind of upset due to this task you could try undertaking the Compassionate Self-Soothing task or the Clearing a Space task that you have learned in the previous chapter.

Once you are ready to proceed, please review the narrative examples of Timothy and Alice in Boxes 3.1 and 3.2, as they recount their own experiences of completing the Overcoming Self-Interruption task. When you have reviewed the same, you can then proceed to complete the Summary Sheet provided in this section (Box 3.3) to record your own experience of this experiential task.

Box 3.1

Overcoming Self-Interruption Task (Summary of Experience: Timothy)

What Timothy was doing during the Overcoming Self-Interruption Task

I know that I avoid talking about how I'm feeling to most of the people I'm close to in my life. My mum was asking me recently how I was doing since the breakup with Rachel and I made a joke about how a global pandemic was a great time to be single (Stage 1). In the Interrupter-Chair I was saying things like (Stage 2): *"laugh it off, it's not worth it, she won't understand, change the subject. Don't get upset, don't embarrass yourself, don't make a big deal."*

In the Experiencer-Chair I was feeling quite cut off, silenced almost (Stage 3). The Interrupter made a convincing argument! I told the Interrupter that he was shutting me down, and that I felt unreasonable for having these feelings in the first place. I felt like my concerns weren't important and at the same time that they were too much too handle, like if I shared them, I would mess everything up more. I felt alone. My shoulders were tense, and my throat was constricted. I felt a pain in my jaw from where I was clenching. I told the Interrupter I understood that he was trying to protect me somehow, but I think it was making me feel worse, I need (Stage 4) to feel supported by him to share some of the burden of what I'm going through.

When I got back into the Interrupter-Chair it felt different, like I've been called out. I was saying things like (Stage 5B) *"I'm sorry I'm making it worse, but I'm scared for you. I don't know if it's a good idea to be so open and trusting but I do want you to feel better. I'm only trying to help so if you want me to stop I will"*.

In the Experiencer-Chair it felt nice to hear that the Interrupter wanted me to feel better and had only been trying to help (Stage 6B). I got it now, what he was trying to achieve, and I appreciated that he was scared about being more open because I am too. I tried to let some of that wash over me and felt the pain in my jaw lessen. I took a deep breath and tried to relax my shoulders a bit too. I told the Interrupter it felt good to know that he cared enough to want to protect me.

Box 3.2

Overcoming Self-Interruption Task (Summary of Experience: Alice)

What Alice was doing during the Overcoming Self-Interruption task

I am afraid of expressing my vulnerable feelings of hurt to my mother-in-law (Stage 1). I would block myself by keeping myself busy with watching movies in my room.

When I was in the Interrupter-Chair (Stage 2), I said that *"there is no point in baring your heart out to your mother-in-law because she doesn't care about how you feel since you are not her biological daughter. She is also not capable of listening to your feelings because talking about feelings has always been a taboo in traditional Asian families"*. I said to myself things like: *"You are being too needy, and you shouldn't expect everyone to love you. You should keep yourself occupied by watching movies in your room to avoid any contact with your mother-in-law. Hold your breath, don't breathe, tilt your head up to hold back your tears and to fortify your heart by numbing it. Don't be a fool. You need to guard your heart by not showing your vulnerabilities to people who are incapable of taking care of your vulnerabilities. If you show your mother-in-law that you are hurt, she may reject you even more for being needy."*

When I switched to the Experiencer-Chair (Stage 3), I felt sad and helpless, like I was all alone in a dark room and there is nobody there for me. I felt suffocated and tensed. My throat felt tight and dry, like the Interrupter was trying to strangle me, and I couldn't breathe. I needed (Stage 4) the Interrupter to understand how I feel and stop her blocking my feelings.

As the Interrupter, I knew you (the Self in the Experiencer-Chair) felt bad, and I felt sorry for you that you felt this way (Stage 5B). I wished to protect the Self in the Experiencer-Chair from these painful feelings. I felt like I can't let go of interrupting (Stage 5A), because I am worried that if you tell your mother-in-law that you need her love and she rejects you, then it will really confirm that you are unlovable. Therefore, I said to the Self in the Experiencer-Chair: *"I will keep interrupting you"*.

As the Self in the Experiencer-Chair, I responded (Stage 6A): *"I need to be free to feel what I feel. I need you* (the Interrupter) *to validate and accept my feelings"*. I felt relieved in being able to share what I need. I felt a little lighter and I could breathe more easily. I said to the Interrupter: *"If you continue to block me, I will ignore you and just validate my own feelings"*. The tightening sensation in my throat has eased up a little and I feel more empowered.

Box 3.3

Summary Sheet: Overcoming Emotional Avoidance (The Self-Interrupter)

Parts Enacted in the Experiencer-Chair	*Parts Enacted in the Interrupter-Chair*
	How do I stop myself from feeling? (Increasing awareness about the ways in which I interrupt myself) _____ _____ _____ _____ _____
	What drives my efforts to stop my feelings? What are my underlying fears that drive those efforts? _____ _____ _____ _____ _____
What impact does the interruption have? What is the personal cost of interruption to me? _____ _____ _____ _____	
What do I need in the face of the interruption? _____ _____ _____ _____ _____	

What do I feel towards the impacted part of me? What reminders of compassionate experiences can help me let go of the interrupting process?

_____

_____

_____

_____

_____

How can I face the interruption? What points can help me remember how I faced the Interrupter in this task and allowed myself to express my emotions?

_____

_____

_____

_____

_____

Note: Remember that you do not need to undertake all the tasks at one time or in one sitting. Please feel free to attend to these tasks in your own time. You can always look up the completed examples from this chapter for Timothy and Alice in Appendix III (pages 162–163) if you need further guidance, clarification, or reference about how to undertake the task.

Quiz for Self-Assessment (See Appendix III, page 164 for Answers)

	True	False
1 Interruption of emotions helps us avoid our feared emotional experiences but can cause us to feel constricted and unexpressed.	☐	☐
2 Some of the ways in which we avoid our emotions include using strategies such as distraction, worrying, and use of substances.	☐	☐
3 The Overcoming Self-Interruption task is useful to undertake when you are feeling afraid of expressing some of your feelings.	☐	☐
4 The Overcoming Self-Interruption task is useful to undertake when you catch yourself wanting to avoid your feelings.	☐	☐
5 The Overcoming Self-Interruption task is a useful way to overcome Self-Criticism.	☐	☐
6 If feeling distressed after doing the Overcoming Self-Interruption task, it may be helpful to undertake the Clearing a Space task.	☐	☐

Note

1 The description of the self-interruption task as used in psychotherapy was described in an early EFT book by Greenberg et al. (1993).

Chapter 4

Overcoming Emotional Avoidance (The Self-Worrier)

Learning Goals

1 To continue building on the learnings about emotional avoidance.
2 To learn an experiential task that is focused on a form of emotional avoidance, called self-worrying (i.e., learning to overcome the Self-Worrier).
3 To use this experiential task to be able to feel and express important emotional experiences, rather than avoiding them by self-worrying, and using such understanding to better inform your actions and behaviours.

Suggested duration: One week

Introduction

This chapter seeks to help you become aware of and learn to interact with your inner self-worrier, which is that inner voice that tries to worry and scare you about upcoming events or situations. Worrying often causes us to overprepare for potential threats (triggers). Excessive worrying results in exhaustion and constant anxiety, which can then lead to avoiding difficult situations which potentially undermines your confidence in managing them over time. The main task of this chapter is to outline a practice known as 'Overcoming the Self-Worrier'. Learning this practice can help you overcome worrying strategies that want us to be prepared for potentially painful feelings but evoke anxiety. In worrying we engage with potential scenarios that could bring painful feelings. We engage with these scenarios in order to be better prepared for them but in reality, the constant worrying about them brings anxiety and tiredness. Worrying is a form of self-protection against feelings we do not want to have. For instance, if I worry about a social situation in which I can be judged, I engage with the possibility of being judged (I worry) because I want to prepare for this option. The worrying elicits anxiety, but really the underlying painful feeling that I want to prevent by preparing for the situation is the shame I would feel if I was judged. Paradoxically, being judged would be more painful than the anxiety I may feel when I am preparing in my head for possible judgement (self-worrying). Thus, worrying (and anxiety) is better than feeling the shame that may be my particular sensitivity (vulnerability). Furthermore, worrying may lead to avoiding social situations altogether so I would not be judged. It thus leads to behavioural avoidance of situations that would bring unbearable painful feelings.

Pre-Task Requirements: In this task, you will role-play and bring into contact two opposing parts of yourself: the self-worrying part and the experiencing self. Both these

DOI: 10.4324/9781003201861-5

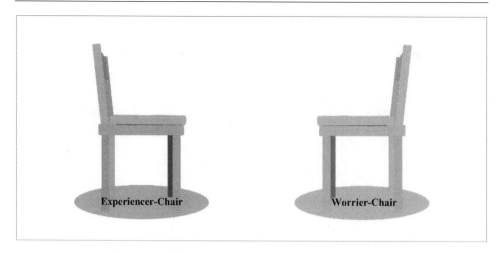

Figure 4.1 Chair positions for the Overcoming Self-Worry task. Experiencer-Chair is on the left side and Worrier-Chair is on the right side.

opposing parts would sit on different chairs. Therefore, for this task, you will need two chairs: your own chair on the left (called the Experiencer-Chair) and an empty chair placed opposite to your chair on the right (called the Worrier-Chair). The two chairs should be facing each other. See Figure 4.1 for reference.

Description of Main Stages of the 'Overcoming the Self-Worrier' Task

In this section we briefly explain the main steps that are involved in this task. This is helpful to prepare you for the task and provide the rationale behind it. Please note that you don't need to undertake instruction steps at this time. You will be provided with detailed guidance sheets in this chapter that are designed to be used when you are ready to undertake the task. Use this section only as an educational piece to help you become familiar with what to expect in the task and use the detailed guidance sheets when you are ready to practice the task.

When to use the task: Normally you will use this task at the moment when you catch yourself worrying about something. You may try it out at first by remembering a situation (an issue) that brought about worrying for you. Throughout this task, remember to focus on your feelings and emotions, rather than on your thoughts. Remember also to take as much time as you need to complete the stages.

Number of Stages: There are six main stages in the Overcoming the Self-Worrier task, as explained in the following:

Stage 1 – Describing Worries

You will begin this task seated in the Experiencer-Chair on the left side. In this first step you will be asked to take a moment to reflect about some of the situations in which you tend to worry or about which you may have been worrying recently. Please select a specific situation that might feel particularly relevant for you or that is more vivid for you in the current moment.

Stage 2 – Enacting the Worrier

In Stage 2, you will be asked to move to the Worrier-Chair and to enact how you tend to worry yourself. Here you will try and be that voice inside of you that produces worries. You will be asked to talk to the Self in the Experiencer-Chair as if you were talking to a person (it will be like two parts of you are having a dialogue, with an internal conversation). For example, being the worrying part, you may tell the Self in the Experiencer-Chair that *"something will go wrong, things won't turn out right, something bad is going to happen, etc."* You will be asked to act the Worrier part and make the Self part worried. As you will visualize yourself in the Experiencer-Chair, you will be guided to say/enact out loud exactly how you express all those worries in your head. Try and not hold back and be as accurate as you can be in voicing out all your worries to the Self part. In this step, try and speak in the tone that best resembles how intense your worries tend to get. This may require you to adopt tones that may express a sense of agitation, insistence, urgency, control, etc. The main element is that you try and enact that Worrier's voice as accurately as you can. Just try and be that voice inside which expresses these worries. As you voice out all these worries to yourself in the Experiencer-Chair, it is important to remind yourself that this IS how you worry yourself internally. In this stage please also try and observe what shape your worries take.

Stage 3 - Experiencing the Impact of the Worrying

In Stage 3, after you have clearly enacted the worrying part of yourself, you will be asked to swap chairs again and to sit in the Experiencer-Chair. Here you will be guided to reflect on how such worrying (that you just heard from the Worrier) affects your internal experience and how it makes you feel. Then you will be guided to articulate what emotional impact the Worrier has (it usually brings anxiety and tiredness) and to express these feelings to the Worrier part on the Worrier-Chair.

Stage 4 – Expressing Unmet Needs

In Stage 4 (still in the Experiencer-Chair), you will be asked to articulate what you need from the Worrier and express this need directly to the Worrier as if they were sitting opposite you and were a different person (e.g., *I need a break from you*).

Stage 5 – Probing for Compassion from the Worrier

This next stage starts once you have clearly expressed to the Worrier how all the worrying affects your internal experience and what you need from the worrier. Thereafter you will be guided to come back to the Worrier-Chair and once again be that part of you that produces worries (Worrier). The Worrier will now be guided to see what their response to the Self is here-and-now after they heard how impacted the Self is and what they need. At this stage, three things can happen:

1 The Worrier wants to continue worrying: If the Worrier is unable to let go of the worrying (producing worries) and feels like continuing the worrying, you will be guided to continue the task with Stage 5(A). **OR**

2 The Worrier wants to stop worrying but does not know how to do so: If the Worrier wants to let go of the worrying but is unable to do so, you will be guided to continue the task with Stage 5(A). **OR**

3 The Worrier wants to let go of the worrying: If the Worrier (the part of you that produces worries) is being understanding and wants to let go of the worrying, you will be guided to continue the task through Stage 5(B).

Note: When you reach this point in the task, it is important to select the most appropriate pathway to continue on with. Stage 5(A) will help you when the Worrier is still unwilling to let go or wants to let go but doesn't know how to do so. Alternatively, Stage 5(B) will help when the Worrier is willing to cooperate and is willing to let go of the worrying.

Stage 6 – Reflecting and Building Boundaries

Based on your experience in Stage 5, you will now be directed to complete the task either via Stage 6(A) or Stage 6(B). If previously the Worrier didn't soften or wouldn't let go of the worrying, now in Stage 6(A) you will be asked to sit in the Experiencer-Chair and see whether you can put a boundary to the relentless Worrier (will you let him/her scare you?). Alternatively, if previously the Worrier did soften, tried to let go, and expressed concern for the Self part, in Stage 6(B) you will be asked to sit in the Experiencer-Chair and let in this softening and see how it feels inside to get it. In case it is a mixture of the two, complete Stage 6(A) first and then proceed to Stage 6(B).

As before, please do not worry about remembering all the stages described here, as the guidance sheets will give you clear instructions about what to do in every stage of the task. You can also download the guidance sheets from the accompanying Support Material (www.routledge.com/9781032063393), print them out and use them for easy and quick reference.

Overcoming the Self-Worrier Guidance Sheets

STAGE I

DESCRIBING WORRIES
(Seating Position: on the <u>Experiencer-Chair</u> to the left)

--

1 Please begin by being seated comfortably on the Experiencer-Chair.
2 Take a moment to think about an emotionally important situation or issue about which you tend to worry or about which you worry now or worried recently.
3 Please select a specific situation that might feel particularly relevant for you or that is perhaps more vivid for you in this current moment.
4 Please proceed to Stage 2 when you are ready.

STAGE 2

ENACTING THE WORRIER
(Seating Position: on the <u>Worrier-Chair</u> on the right)

--

1   Please move to the Worrier-Chair and enact how you worry yourself.
2   Be that voice inside of you as if it was the person that is making somebody else worried and speak to the Self that you imagine in the other, Experiencer-Chair.
3   Try and make the Self worried by expressing those worrying thoughts. For instance, tell the Self about all the things that can go wrong.
4   As you visualize the Self in the Experiencer-Chair opposite to you, worry the Self, say out loud to the Self part all the things that might go wrong in the situation that you have select.
5   Try to be as accurate in voicing out all your worries to the Self part and try not to hold back.
6   Continue to express all your worries to the Self part on the Experiencer-Chair. This may cause you to adopt tones that may express a sense of agitation, insistence, urgency, control, and/or upset.
7   The main thing to remember is to be as accurate as you can in expressing the voice inside that constantly worries. Remember that this IS how you worry yourself internally.
8   Take as much time as you need to complete this stage. When you are ready, please proceed to Stage 3.

STAGE 3

EXPERIENCING THE IMPACT OF WORRYING
(Seating Position: on the <u>Experiencer-Chair</u> to the left)

--

1   Now, when you feel that you have clearly enacted the worrying in the Worrier-Chair, return back to the Experiencer-Chair and become the part of you that is impacted by the worrying.

2   As you sit in the Experiencer-Chair, try to feel how the Worrier's constant worrying affects your internal experience. How does it feel inside? What is your sense when you get this from the Worrier?

3   Take a breath and see how it feels inside. What happens inside when you get this flow of worries? Often people feel anxious or tired but see how you feel yourself. Try to name the feelings for yourself.

4   As you name the feelings for yourself, tell them to the Worrier (as if it was a real person sitting in the other chair). Also tell the Worrier how you feel when he/she worries you? Tell the Worrier what it is like for you to hear all this worrying.

5   Even though some of the worries may have felt like being 'true' for you, try to stay with the feelings they evoke in you. No matter how 'true' the worries might seem, it must also be very unpleasant to hear so many worrying thoughts, right?

6   Often, it can get so exhausting, overwhelming, and can bring so much anxiety to have all this flow of constant worrying. How does the worrying make you feel inside?

7   Try to notice any physical sensations that may be happening within your body. Notice this especially when the Worrier tends to go on and on, all the time with all these worries. What is the impact of that on your body?

8   Can you voice out the feelings from that part of your body, where the worrying impacts you most and tell the Worrier how you feel when the Worrier gives you all those worrying thoughts?

9   Take as much time as you need. When you have thoroughly expressed yourself to the Worrier about how the worrying impacts you, proceed to Stage 4.

STAGE 4

EXPRESSING UNMET NEEDS
(Seating Position: on the <u>Experiencer-Chair</u> to the left)

--

1   Continue to be seated in the Experiencer-Chair.
2   Now begin to think about what the feelings that were evoked by the Worrier need. What do you need from the Worrier as you feel all this inside? For instance, this could be something like "*I need you to be quiet*" and "*I need you to just let me be*".
3   Try to voice out what you feel you need from the Worrier. First name these for your-self, then say it to the Worrier: "*I need you to…*"
4   Take as much time as you need to express to the Worrier what you need from it.
5   When you are ready, please proceed to Stage 5.

STAGE 5

PROBING FOR COMPASSION FROM THE WORRIER
(Seating Position: on the <u>Worrier-Chair</u> on the right)

--

1   Now please move to the Worrier-Chair.
2   Now being the Worrier part, what do you feel towards the feelings and needs that were expressed by the Self part in the other Experiencer-Chair? What do you feel towards the Self part that creates so much upset and distress by all your constant worrying? What do you feel towards the Self?
3   Tell the Self part how you feel towards them.
4   Can you see the impact of your worries? Would you now wish to let go of some of these worries, or do you feel even more scared that if you let go, the Self part would be unprotected, and you would continue to feel like worrying him or her more? See what fits more. Sometimes it can also be a mixture of the two. Based on how you are feeling, choose <u>one</u> of the options from below:

Choose one of the most appropriate options below from 5(A) or 5(B).

5(A) Wanting to Continue Worrying Further or Mixture of Feelings

1   If this is the case, try to identify what makes it difficult to let go of your worrying. Sometimes, you may event want to do so but you may be unable to.
2   Say that you will keep worrying the Self part and tell him or her what drives your worries (for instance, to make sure that nothing bad would ever happen). Express this to the Self part on the Experiencer-Chair: *"I can't let go of the worrying because…."* Or *"My worrying is fully automated so I am feeling like I cannot let go of it"*.
3   Also say that you will keep worrying the Self on the Experiencer-Chair: *"I will keep on worrying you…"*
4   At this stage, the Worrier may not be willing or able to let go of the worries. It may have told you why and insisted on worrying you more. If this is the case, continue the task using Stage 6(A).
5   In case that the Worrier wanted to let go of the worrying but was unable to do so or was ambivalent about letting go of worrying (or still continuing with), please complete this stage (5A) and then also 5B (below). After that, go through Stage 6 (A) and then proceed to Stage 6 (B).

-Go now to Stage 6(A)-

5(B) Wanting to Let Go of the Worrying

1   As the Worrier, you may see the impact of your constant worrying and feel for the Self on the Experiencer-Chair, and you may feel like letting go of your worrying.

2   Please take some time to express this feeling of wanting to let go of (over) protecting and letting go of the constant worrying of the Self in the Experiencer-Chair.

3   At this stage, you may have heard the Worrier be somewhat compassionate towards the Self in the Experiencer-Chair and wanting to let go of the worrying. If this is the case, continue on with Stage 6(B).

-Go now to Stage 6(B)-

Note: When you reach this point in the task, it is important to select the most appropriate pathway to continue on with. Stage 6(A) will help you when the Worrier is still unwilling to let go. Alternatively, Stage 6(B) will help you when the Worrier is willing to cooperate with the Experiencer and is willing to let go of the worrying. In case it is a mixture of the two, complete Stage 6(A) first and then proceed to Stage 6(B).

STAGE 6(A)

REFLECTING AND BUILDING BOUNDARIES
(Seating Position: on the <u>Experiencer-Chair</u> to the left)

--

1   Please return to the Experiencer-Chair.
2   So, there is no willingness on the Worrier part to try to let go of the worrying even when the Worrier sees how it impacts you. The Worrier is perhaps persuaded that worrying will protect you or the Worrier is too scared to let go of the worrying.
3   So how does it impact you now here, when you hear the Worrier determined to worry you further? What is your response to such determination to be in charge of you and worry you? Do you like it? What is it that you really need for yourself?
4   Will you allow the Worrier to take such control over you? If not, tell the Worrier what you will do if he/she keeps on worrying you. Make sure that you follow what you really need. If you are unable to stand up to the Worrier at this stage, express to the Worrier what you would do if you had more power.
5   How does it feel when you say what you need, what you will do in the face of the Worrier if he/she keeps worrying you? What is it like to stand up for yourself? You may have felt more confident about yourself, or felt some relief? Tell the Worrier how you feel when you stand up for yourself.
6   What will be your response to the Worrier if it keeps doing the relentless worrying? Tell the Worrier what your response would be.
7   Now, take a moment to pause and reflect on how you feel when you express to the Worrier what you will do. See how it feels inside to express yourself and to stand up for yourself.
8   Take a few deep breaths.
9   Well-done. You have now completed the required task.

STAGE 6(B)

LETTING IN SOFTENING
(Seating Position: on the <u>Experiencer-Chair</u> to the left)

--

1 Please return to the Experiencer-Chair.
2 So, there seems to be some understanding coming from the Worrier towards you. How is it to hear those softer words? Can you try to let some of it in? How does it feel inside?
3 You may not even yet believe those understanding words and may not trust them. But just for a moment, could you check inside and see how it feels to be told by the Worrier that they would want to let go of the worry, and they see what impact the worrying has on you?
4 Now, tell the Worrier how it feels for you inside to receive that sense of understanding and compassion.
5 Now, take a moment to pause and reflect on how you feel when the Worrier expressed that they would want to let go of their worrying. See how it feels inside and take a few deep breaths. Name the feeling you feel now on the reception of the Worrier's attempt to let go.
6 Name this for yourself and then express it to the Worrier.
7 Take a few deep breaths.
8 Well-done. You have now completed the required task.

Overcoming Avoidance (Self-Worrier) – Summary

This chapter built on the learnings of the previous chapter and introduced an additional form of problematic self-relating, i.e., the self-worrier. Self-worrying is a strategy that gives us a sense that we are doing something (i.e., worrying) to prevent painful feelings and potentially also the situation that could evoke them. Yet such worrying comes at a high cost. Worrying can make us feel overwhelmed, exhausted, anxious, and can also make us feel tense in our bodies. Hopefully, through attempting the task in this chapter, you have become more aware of how you may be growing your anxiety and at the same time avoiding feeling other painful feelings through worrying. Learning to let go of worrying can help you gain more self-confidence and allow you more space to fully feel what you are experiencing in different situations, it frees you up to consider your thoughts, behaviours, and actions. If you are feeling any kind of upset due to undertaking this task, remember that you could try undertaking the Compassionate Self-Soothing task or the Clearing a Space task that you have learned in Chapter 2.

Once you are ready to proceed, please review the narrative examples of Timothy and Alice in Boxes 4.1 and 4.2, as they recount their own experiences of completing the Overcoming Self-Worrier task. When you have reviewed the same, you can then proceed to complete the Summary Sheet provided in this section (Box 4.3) to record your own experience of this experiential task.

Box 4.1

Overcoming Self-Worrier Task (Summary of Experience: Timothy)

What Timothy was doing during the Overcoming Self-Worrier task

I was thinking about my situation in work. In the Worrier-Chair I was saying things like (Stage 2): *"If you don't get a hold of yourself, you're going to get fired, everybody thinks you're terrible at your job. You used to be able to manage so much better than this, but you are just not able. If you lose your job you'll have to move out of your house and back in with your mum, you'll never meet someone living at home. You'll probably never meet someone again anyways; Rachel was a one of a kind and you messed it up with her. You're just not cut out to be in relationships and you'll end up alone."* I sounded agitated and fast paced, like I couldn't get the worries out quick enough.

Sitting in the Experiencer-Chair (Stage 3) I felt like I couldn't catch my breath, my shoulders were tense like there was a ton of bricks resting on my shoulders. The pressure was intense, and it made me feel stuck and helpless like there was nothing I could do to resolve or release it. I started to feel deflated and exhausted. I told the Worrier that I felt panicky and powerless when he worried me. I told him that he was relentless and exhausting and that he was getting in the way of what's important to me. He was getting in my head and distracting me from being able to do the job I want. I told him I need (Stage 4) him to shut up, to quieten down, to just give me a break! I'm surprised by how forcefully I say these things and feel them.

In the Worrier-Chair I was feeling a bit shocked (Stage 5). I said things like *"I didn't realise how damaging I was being, I was only trying to protect you from the things you fear. I care about you; I know you work hard and that's the only reason I think and say the things I do. I don't want you to fail, I want you to succeed. I want to stop; I will quieten down."* (Stage 5B)

As the Self part I was trying to let this sentiment in (Stage 6B); I was relieved that there was a part of me that wanted me to succeed but I was annoyed that he (the Worrier) had been so present for so long and I was a little sceptical that he would be able to shut up. I took a few deep breathes and tried to imagine what it would be like without all the worrying, how much more energy and space I would have on a day-to-day basis. How much more enjoyable things would feel again. I told the Worrier that it feels good to be on the same page, that already I feel calmer and less exhausted. I told him I needed him to stick to this agreement and that I wouldn't be afraid to put him in his place again if he slips up (Stage 6A). I feel strong in myself saying this out loud.

Box 4.2

Overcoming Self-Worrier Task (Summary of Experience: Alice)

What Alice was doing during the Overcoming Self-Worrier task

In the Worrier-Chair (Stage 2) I expressed things like: "*If you don't step up at work, people will eventually find out that you are an imposter. Your colleagues may be talking behind your back that you do less work than others yet get paid more than them. However, if you do more at work, your husband and son will resent you for prioritizing work over them. This year is a crucial year for your son since he will be sitting for his primary school leaving examinations. If you don't supervise him closely, he will be too distracted by his online gaming and he will fail his examinations. If he repeats his year, his self-esteem will suffer a huge blow and it will be even harder for him to make friends because he is falling behind them.*

As I sat in the Experiencer-Chair (Stage 3), I felt stressed and pressurized. It felt like a ton of weight was pressing against my chest and I couldn't breathe properly. I felt anxious and helpless. I said to the Worrier: "*When you worry me I feel even more stressed and fearful. I am so paralyzed by this anxiety that I can't get started on doing anything. When you give me all these worrying thoughts, the impact on my body is that I feel so overwhelmed and exhausted. I am noticing tension in my chest and head. I need you (Stage 4) to just go away and leave me alone.*"

As I sit in the Worrier-Chair (Stage 5), I express: "*I feel concern for you that what I said has caused you so much distress and physical problems (Stage 5B). I don't mean to hurt you and I want the best for you. However, I can't go away because my worries are real. I'm scared that if I stop warning you of what is likely going to happen, you will not be prepared for what is to come. I can't let go and I will keep worrying you (the Self in the Experiencer-Chair) because I want you to be fully prepared so that you won't be left all alone (Stage 5A).*"

As I sat in the Experiencer-Chair, I tried to let in the concern from the Worrier (Stage 6B). I felt slightly more relieved that at least the Worrier now knows the extent of distress the worries have caused me. It feels comforting to hear that the Worrier cares about how I feel. "*Thank you for acknowledging the impact of the worries on me. However, when you said you will continue to worry me, I feel annoyed at you (Stage 6A). I don't like to be controlled by you all the time. I need a break from you and your worries. I need to feel appreciated for trying my best. I don't have enough strength to stand up to you, but if I had more power, I would walk away from you and do what I deem is enough, instead of doing what you think is best for me.*"

I feel more empowered now I have expressed what I need. It's like a warm energy coming up from my chest. I said: "*I feel lighter and more relaxed when I stood up to you. If you keep scaring me and controlling me with your relentless worrying, I will walk away from you and treat everything you say as rubbish. I feel like a heavy weight has lifted from my chest.*"

Box 4.3

Summary Sheet: Overcoming Worrying (The Self-Worrier)

Parts Enacted in the Experiencer-Chair	Parts Enacted in the Worrier-Chair
	How do I worry myself? (Increasing awareness of the ways you worry yourself): _____ _____ _____ _____
	What drives my worries? (Try to focus on the underlying fears that worrying tries to prevent to be fulfilled) _____ _____ _____ _____ _____
What impact does the worrying have? What is the emotional, physical, and personal cost to me? _____ _____ _____ _____	
What do I need in the face of the worry? (Articulating the need with regards to the worry) _____ _____ _____ _____ _____	

What do I feel towards the impacted part of me? (Bringing a reminder of compassionate experiences that may help let go of the worry)

_____

_____

_____

_____

How can I face the worrying? What points can help me remember how I faced the Worrier in this task and allowed myself to express my emotions?

_____

_____

_____

_____

_____

Note: Remember that you do not need to undertake all the tasks at one time or in one sitting. Please feel free to attend to these tasks in your own time. You can always look up the completed examples from this chapter for Timothy and Alice in Appendix IV (pages 165–166) if you need further guidance, clarification, or reference about how to undertake the task.

Quiz for Self-Assessment (See Appendix IV, page 167 for Answers)

		True	False
1	Self-Worrying and Self-Interruption are two strategies that people use to avoid their emotions.	☐	☐
2	Feeling tired, exhausted, and anxious are the most typical experiences of persons impacted by Self-Worrying.	☐	☐
3	Worrying often causes us to overprepare for potential threats.	☐	☐
4	Worrying is a form of self-protection against feelings that we do not want to have.	☐	☐
5	Worrying can lead to avoidance of situations that would bring unbearable painful feelings.	☐	☐
6	After completing any experiential task, it can be useful to do the Clearing a Space task or the Compassionate Self-Soothing task.	☐	☐

Chapter 5

Transforming the Self-Critic

Learning Goals

1 To bring our focus to the learning processes that can transform our longstanding painful feelings into more productive emotional experiences.
2 To enhance our understanding about how we criticize ourselves and consider the impact of such criticism on our emotional experiences.
3 To learn an experiential task that is focused on responding to such self-criticisms and moving towards the transformation of the Self-Critic.

Suggested duration: One week

Introduction

In this chapter and the next, we will be focusing on two processes that can transform our longstanding painful feelings into more helpful and tolerable emotional experiences. There are two main emotion-focused tasks used to bring about such transformative emotional experiences. These are the 'Self-to-Self' dialogue task focusing on the problematic self-criticism, and the 'Self-to-Other' dialogue task focusing on transforming interpersonal emotional injuries. In this chapter we will focus on the 'Self-to-Self' task, which is a two-chair dialogue task used for transforming problematic self-criticism.

   Many of us experience an internal, critical voice which often leads to painful and self-defeating feelings. We often criticize ourselves in order to improve and be better in our achievements or to improve how we are seen by others or to uphold our internal standards for ourselves. It is a natural and adaptive process of self-adjustment. It often emerges from developmentally important periods in our life (e.g., childhood, adolescence, etc.). We want to have good qualities that would be considered as such by others. Unfortunately, at times we can receive reactions from others that conflict with what we hope for. Consequently, we may start to push ourselves more (e.g., to be better, kinder, smarter…, etc.) with the belief that this will result in our desired outcome (e.g., to be accepted, worthy, loved…, etc.). In this way we can develop a maladaptive self-criticism. At other times we may internalize a problematic criticism from the criticisms directed at us by people who are authority figures (e.g., parents, teachers, older siblings…, etc.). Potentially adaptive processes of self-adjustment can therefore develop into a disproportionate maladaptive self-criticism. Such self-criticism may elicit painful feelings of shame that are unbearable, and we

DOI: 10.4324/9781003201861-6

may fall into hopelessness and helplessness, or start to find ourselves dreading further self-criticism.

In this chapter we will focus on how we criticize ourselves and consider what impact this has on our emotional experience. We will consider the various ways in which we can respond to self-criticism so that we can meet our emotional needs as they become highlighted by the impact of the criticism we experience. We will also look at whether we are able to be accepting of ourselves and have a more self-compassionate stance.

Transforming the Self-Critic

As we outlined earlier, the internal 'Self-Critic' has several functions. For instance, it may be an effort to shape ourselves constructively, so that we are positively regarded by others (e.g., *"my father will be proud of me if I become a better daughter"*). Internal criticisms might also be attempts at avoiding the fear of losing desired qualities (e.g., *"If I don't excel in life, then nobody will want to be with me"*). They may also be an internalization of the perceived judgement of other people (e.g., *"They don't like spending time with me, so I must be weird or unlovable"*).

As we can see from these examples, problematic self-criticism is often our attempt to improve ourselves. However, such a strategy doesn't help when instead of feeling motivated towards a goal, we end up instead feeling put down, ashamed, embarrassed, worthless, and resigned to feeling like *"I am not good enough!"*. Sadly, even though this inner voice can be critical and vicious at times, we can also actively seek it out when we start to believe we 'deserve' such self-punishment. Paradoxically, for some of us, we may even feel relief through engaging in this kind of self-critical behaviour. Over time this can lead to the unintended unhelpful consequence of feeling attached to our self-critic, and consequently feel less able to shift the feelings of worthlessness and the shame associated with it. Therefore, it is very important that we try to tackle such inner self-criticism as soon as we start to become aware of the potential unhelpful effect it is having over us.

The Transforming the Self-Critic task allows you to access core painful feelings such as shame elicited by self-criticism. The goal of this task is to allow you to be able to counter the experience of self-criticism and shame with emotional experiences such as feeling proud of your own personal qualities, feeling loved, feeling appreciated, feeling accepted, and being able to set healthy boundaries to the critic (i.e., having an ability for healthy assertiveness). The imaginary and experiential nature of this task makes it evocative with the aim of enabling an authentic experience of having a realistic dialogue. Therefore, it is important that you try to engage with this task as best as you can and not hold back during your expression.

Pre-Task Requirements: In this task, you will real-play and bring into contact two opposing parts of yourself: the inner Critic part and the Experiencing Self part, which is impacted by the criticism. Both of these opposing parts will sit on different chairs. Therefore, for this task, you will need two chairs placed opposite to each other. That is, the two chairs should be facing each other. The chair on the left will be called the Experiencer-Chair, and the chair on the right will be called the Critic-Chair. See Figure 5.1 for reference. Please be seated in the Experiencer-Chair at the start of the task in a comfortable position and begin by focusing on your breathing.

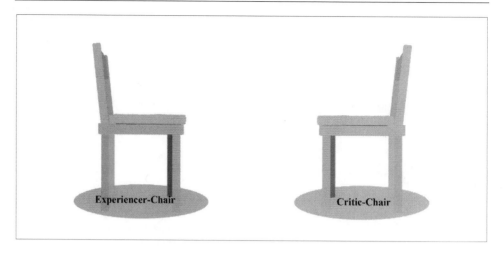

Figure 5.1 Chair positions for the Transforming the Self-Critic task. Experiencer-Chair is on the left side and Critic-Chair is on the right side.

Description of Main Stages of the 'Transforming the Self-Critic' Task

In this section we briefly explain the main steps that are involved in this task. This is helpful to prepare you for the task and provide the rationale behind it. Please note that you don't need to undertake these instructions at this time. You will be provided with detailed guidance sheets in this chapter that are designed to be used when you are ready to undertake the task. Use this section only as an educational piece to help you become familiar with what to expect in the task and use the detailed guidance sheets when you are ready to practice the task.

When to use the task: Normally you will use this task only at the moment when you catch yourself criticizing yourself. You may try it out at first by remembering a situation (an issue) in which you tended to criticize yourself. Throughout this task, remember to focus on your feelings and emotions, rather than on your thoughts. Remember also to take as much time as you need to complete the stages.

Number of stages: There are six main stages in the Overcoming the Self-Critic task, as explained in the following:

Stage 1 – Becoming Aware of the Self-Criticism

In this first stage, you will be asked to take a moment to reflect on some of the situations in which you tend to criticize yourself or are currently self-critical. For instance, think about *the ways* in which you criticize yourself and for *what reasons*? Reflect on situations in which you would likely be self-critical or have been self-critical in the past or are self-critical right now.

Stage 2 – Enactment of the Critic

Once you have thought of a situation in which you criticize yourself, you will be asked to move to the Critic-Chair. Then you will be guided to visualize your Self seated in the chair opposite to you in the Experiencer-Chair. As you visualize your Self in the other chair, you will be required to enact out loud exactly how you criticize yourself in your own mind. You will be asked to tell the Self part in the other chair all that you think (as the Critic) that is wrong with him or her. For example, you may include criticisms such as *"you should have done this [fill in the relevant thing that you criticize yourself for]"*, *"you are stupid"*, *"you are a failure"*, *"you are unworthy"*, or *"you are selfish"*. It may be different criticisms but, in this step, try and reflect on the specific character judgements or personal qualities the Self-Critic is so frustrated with (e.g., *"you are selfish"*).

Stage 3 – Experiencing the Impact of the Criticisms

In Stage 3, once you have clearly enacted the Critic part of yourself, you will be asked to swap chairs again and to now become the Experiencer part of you (in the Experiencer-Chair) which is emotionally impacted by all these criticisms. Here you will be guided to reflect on how such criticism affects your internal experience and how it makes you feel. Then you will be guided towards expressing these feelings to the Critic part on the other Critic-Chair, e.g., *"I feel so diminished when you criticize me, and it aches so much"*.

Stage 4 – Expressing Unmet Needs

As you stay with the emotional impact of the criticism (still in the Experiencer-Chair) you will also be asked to try to articulate what you need from the Critic when you feel so criticized and so emotionally impacted. You will also express to the Critic what you need from them (e.g., *"I need you to give me a break"*).

Stage 5 – Probing for Compassion from the Critic

Once you have clearly expressed to the Critic how all the criticisms impact your internal experience and also expressed what you need from the Critic, you will proceed to Stage 5. In this stage, you will be guided to move back to the Critic-Chair and once again be the Critic part. This Critic part will be guided to express to the Experiencer part on the opposite Experiencer-Chair what they feel (as the Critic) towards the Self when they see the Self in pain and expressing the need towards you (the Critic). At this stage, two things can happen:

1   The Critic wants to continue being critical of the Self and no compassion is coming: If the Critic is unable to let go of the criticisms or wants to continue the criticizing process, you will be guided to continue the task by moving on to **Stage 5(A)**. **OR**
2   The Critic feels some compassion towards the Self and wants to let go of the criticizing: If the Critic is being understanding and experiencing some compassion, and wants to let go of the criticisms, you will be guided to continue the task by moving on to **Stage 5(B)**.

> Note: When you reach this point in the task, it is important to select the most appropriate pathway to continue on with. Stage 6(A) will help you when the Critic is still unwilling to stop criticizing. Alternatively, Stage 6(B) will help you when the Critic is willing to cooperate with the Self and is willing to let go of the criticizing.

Stage 6 – Reflecting and Building Boundaries

In the previous Stage 5, you will be directed to either continue with Stage 6(A) or Stage 6(B). In Stage 6(A), if the Critic won't soften or let go in Stage 5, you will be asked to sit in the Experiencer-Chair and see whether you can put a boundary to the relentless Critic (will you let him/her criticize you?). Alternatively, in Stage 6(B), if the Critic softened (Stage 5B) and tried to let go of criticism and expressed the concern for the Self impacted by the Critic, you will be asked to sit in the Experiencer-Chair and let in this softening/compassion and see how it feels inside to get it.

As before, please do not worry about remembering all the stages described here, as the guidance sheets will give you clear instructions about what to do in every stage of the task. You can read how Timothy and Alice approach this task in Boxes 5.1 and 5.2. When you have reviewed the same, you can then proceed to complete the Summary Sheet provided in this section (Box 5.3) to record your own experience of this experiential task. You can also download a copy of the guidance sheets from the accompanying Support Material (www.routledge.com/9781032063393), print it out, and use for easy and quick reference.

Transforming the Self-Critic Guidance Sheets

STAGE 1

BECOMING AWARE OF THE SELF-CRITICISM
(Seating Position: on the <u>Experiencer-Chair</u> to the left)

--

1 Please be seated on the Experiencer-Chair.
2 Take a moment to reflect on the ways in which you tend to criticize yourself (i.e., criticize yourself in your mind). Consider situations in which you are likely to be self-critical or have been self-critical in the past or more recently, or indeed are currently.
3 When you are ready, proceed with Stage 2.

STAGE 2

ENACTMENT OF THE CRITIC
(Seating Position: on the __Critic-Chair__ on the right)

--

1 Now, please move to the Critic-Chair, and try to visualize yourself, seated in the opposite Experiencer-Chair.

2 As you visualize yourself in the other chair, enact out loud exactly how you criticize yourself in your own head. Speak as if you were talking to the other person (the other person being you in the Experiencer-Chair).

3 Continue to enact the Critic and tell the Self on the opposite chair all that is wrong with him or her. For instance, these may include criticisms such as *"you are stupid"*, *"you are a failure"*, *"you are unworthy"*, or *"you are selfish"*. Think particularly of personal qualities that you negatively judge in yourself.

4 Without holding back, try to be as accurate in voicing out your criticisms, speaking to the Self (i.e., your imagined self on the other Experiencer-Chair) as if it was a separate person. You may speak in the tone best resembling how intense your self-criticisms tend to get.

5 Notice the tone with which you criticize the Self. What are the words that you are using to criticize the Self? What is the tone of your voice?

6 As you voice out all these criticisms against your Self, it is important to realise that this IS how you criticize yourself internally in your own mind.

7 Take as much time as you need to complete this.

8 When you have completed expressing the criticisms, please proceed on to Stage 3.

STAGE 3

EXPERIENCING THE IMPACT OF THE CRITICISMS
(Seating Position: on the <u>Experiencer-Chair</u> to the left)

--

1   Now, when you feel that you have clearly enacted the Critic part, please return to the Experiencer-Chair and become the part of yourself that is impacted by the Critic's judgements.

2   Now, try to see how such criticism affects your internal emotional experience. How does it feel inside to be so criticized? Imagine that the criticism came from another person (although it is just your inner voice).

3   Take a breath and see how it feels for you.

4   Once you have become aware of the emotional impact of the Critic's judgement, express to the Critic how it makes you feel? You may have experienced a whole range of different emotions (feeling attacked, put down, not having enough value, etc.). Tell the Critic what was it is like for you to hear all this criticism?

5   Remember, even though some of the criticisms may have felt 'true' for you, try to stay with the feelings they evoke in you. Try not to be interested in whether the criticism is true or not, just see how it makes you feel.

6   No matter how well they seem to 'fit', it must also be very unpleasant to hear so much criticism, right? It does hurt to be attacked or put down, doesn't it?

7   Can you now tell the Critic how it feels inside when it is criticizing you? Try to notice any physical sensations that may be happening within your body; especially when the Critic speaks so harshly to you? Can you voice out the feelings from that part of your body, where the criticism impacts you most?

8   Take as much time as you need. When you are ready, please proceed to Stage 4.

STAGE 4

EXPRESSING UNMET NEEDS
(Seating Position: on the <u>Experiencer-Chair</u> to the left)

--

1   Now, also tell the Critic what you need from him or her as you feel all this inside. What do you need him or her to do? For instance, this could be something like *"I need you to understand"* or *"I need you to be nicer to me"* or *"I need you to accept me for who I am"*.
2   See for yourself what needs feel right for you.
3   Try to voice out what you really need from the Critic. Take as much time as you need to complete this step.
4   When you are ready, please move on to Stage 5.

STAGE 5

PROBING FOR COMPASSION FROM THE CRITIC
(Seating Position: on the <u>Critic-Chair</u> on the right)

--

1 Please move to the Critic-Chair.
2 Now, as the Critic, what do you feel towards the Self in the Experiencer-Chair? What do you feel towards the part that feels so much hurt by all your criticisms and your relentless negative evaluation? What do you feel towards the Self? Can you see the hurt? Can you see what this part of yourself needs from you?
3 What is your response to the Self part?
4 See whether you can soften and respond with compassion or whether you feel like criticizing more. What is your response?
5 At this stage, consider whether you in the Critic-Chair want to continue criticizing the Self in the Experiencer-Chair (5A) or are willing to let go of the criticisms (5B). See what your response is towards the Self.

Now, choose the most appropriate option from 5(A) <u>or</u> 5(B).

5(A) Wanting to Continue Criticizing

1 If you are unable to respond with compassion, see what prevents you from responding with compassion. Often it is fear that if the critic softened, the Self in the Experiencer-Chair would be even more vulnerable, or not liked by the others. At times, we can't soften as we have learnt to associate compassion with pity and rejection.
2 There may be other reasons why you can't soften. Try to see what they are. What is the function of your criticisms? Try to name it for yourself and express to the Self in the Experiencer-Chair. For example: "*I will criticize you because...*". Please take as much time as you need to do this.
3 Now, please come back to the Experiencer-Chair and continue with **Stage 6(A)** if you in the Critic-Chair had felt unwilling of letting go of the criticisms.

-Go to Stage 6(A)-

5(B) Wanting to Let Go of the Criticisms/Expressing Self-Compassion

1 As the Critic, you may see the impact of the criticisms and feel for the Self and you may feel like letting go of the criticisms. You may also feel compassionate towards the Self in the Experiencer-Chair.
2 Please take some time to express this feeling of wanting to let go of the criticisms of the Self in the Experiencer-Chair or expressing compassion towards the Self.
3 Now please come back the Experiencer-Chair and continue with **Stage 6(B)** if you in the Critic-Chair felt like letting go of the criticisms and were self-compassionate.

-Go to Stage 6(B)-

STAGE 6(A)

REFLECTING AND BUILDING BOUNDARIES
(Seating Position: on the <u>Experiencer-Chair</u> to the left)

--

Remember: Use this Pathway A only if you (earlier as the Critic) had felt unwilling of letting go of the criticisms.

1   Please be seated in the Experiencer-Chair.
2   So, there is no understanding or compassion coming from the Critic part, even when the Critic sees you so hurt and upset. So, what is your response to that, when you hear the Critic say all that to you? Is it okay that the Critic speaks to you like this? Is it acceptable?
3   What is your response to such dismissal of your feelings, and to so little care and understanding for you?
4   It doesn't feel good at all, does it, to hear that Critic part be so uncaring towards your feelings? Will you allow the Critic to keep doing this to you? Can you try to set a boundary to the Critic?
5   It may be difficult to stand up for yourself, but if you were able to do that, what would you want? For example, you might tell the Critic: "*if I was able, I would say to you 'back off and stop criticizing'*".
6   Now tell the Critic what is not okay in how the Critic is with you.
7   How does it feel when you say that? What was it like to stand up for yourself? You may have felt more confident about yourself, or felt some relief? Tell the Critic part how you felt when you stood up for yourself.
8   What will be your response to the Critic part if it keeps doing the relentless criticism of you? Tell the Critic part what your response would be.
9   Now, take a moment to pause and reflect on how you feel inside and take a few deep breaths.
10   Well-done. You have now completed the required task.

STAGE 6(B)

LETTING IN SOFTENING
(Seating Position: on the <u>Experiencer-Chair</u> to the left)

--

Remember: Use this Pathway B only if you (earlier as the Critic) had felt willing to let go of the criticisms and were compassionate.

1   Please be seated on the Experiencer-Chair. There seems to be some understanding coming from the Critic part towards you. How is it to hear those understanding words? Can you try to let some of them in?

2   How does it feel inside? There has been a lot of hurt, and it might be difficult to take all this in. You may not even yet believe those understanding words from the Critic and may cringe at hearing them. But just for a moment, could you check inside, and see how it feels to be told from the Critic part that they feel more understanding and caring towards you.

3   Now, tell the Critic part how it feels for you inside. Tell the Critic how it was to have received those understanding words from them.

4   Now, take a moment to pause and reflect on how you feel inside and take a few deep breaths.

5   Well-done. You have now completed the required task.

Transforming the Self-Critic – Summary

Well-done on completing the Transforming the Self-Critic task. Hopefully, you would have experienced a shift in your emotional experience of your self-critic. However, it might have felt quite difficult to do this task. If this was the case, it could be good to try the Compassionate Self-Soothing task from Chapter 2 to help you regulate any distress that you may be experiencing. Alternatively, you may consider undertaking the Clearing a Space task, also from Chapter 2.

In this chapter we learnt how to work towards transforming the self-critic so that we can reduce the painful and self-defeating feelings that it can bring and strengthen productive support for yourself. We also learnt that problematic self-criticism tends to serve several functions, for example to improve ourselves or feel positively regarded by others. However, sometimes such strategies do not help us in the long term, and we end up feeling quite put down, ashamed, embarrassed, and worthless.

One of the hardest parts of this task, and one of the most helpful take away points, is often noticing how you and your self-critic are not one and the same. The Critic is a *powerful aspect* of yourself, but *it is not all of who you are.* You may have noticed a more compassionate and encouraging voice in the dialogue task and it's important to remember that this alternative voice is just as much a part of you as the Critic. They may be quieter at times, but it is your job to nurture this voice too, and this becomes easier when we notice the emotional benefits of listening to it instead of the Critic all the time. We recommend that you engage in 'Transforming the Self-Critic' repeatedly over the next few weeks. You may notice that it is becoming easier to stand up to or soften the Critic as necessary.

Once you are ready to proceed, please review the narrative examples of Timothy and Alice in Boxes 5.1 and 5.2, as they recount their own experiences of completing the Transforming the Self-Critic task. When you have reviewed the same, you can then proceed to complete the Summary Sheet provided in this section (Box 5.3) to record your own experience of this experiential task.

Remember: If you are feeling any kind of upset due to this task you could try undertaking the Compassionate Self-Soothing task or the Clearing a Space task that you have previously learnt in Chapter 2.

Box 5.1

Transforming the Self-Critic Task (Summary of Experience: Timothy)

What Timothy was doing during the Transforming the Self-Critic task

I've been spending more and more time in the evenings going over the breakup in my head. I feel like such an awful person for hurting Rachel (Stage 1), for telling her I didn't want to move in with her. She was so upset and hurt. I didn't have the courage to tell her how unsure of myself I am right now, and how different things seem for her. In the Critic-Chair (Stage 2) I was saying things like "*You're so stupid you couldn't even explain how you felt, you've ruined your chance. You weren't good enough for her, she's better off without you – just like your dad – look how much happier he is without you. You're failing at everything right now, you're an outsider and a complete slob and it's only a matter of time before you'll have to move back in with your mum. You're pathetic.*" I sounded cold and measured, like I really believed everything I was saying.

In the Experiencer-Chair (Stage 3) I felt taut and wounded, like I had been physically shoved into the seat I was sitting in. I felt inadequate like I was back standing in front of the class for spelling test all those years ago. I told the Critic how hard it is to hear those things; how hard it is not to believe them. It makes me feel like I'm completely worthless, and like there's no point trying to get better at any of it. I felt stranded and alone and miserable. I told the Critic how painful it is to hear these judgements levelled against me, how I felt the need to wrap my arms around myself to physically withstand them. I told the Critic that: I need (Stage 4) him to know the pain he is causing me; I need him to understand how unbearable it is to hear those things having been shunned and bullied by others my whole life. I told the Critic how I needed to be accepted by him more than anyone else, I needed him on my side, and I felt tears on my cheeks as I said this.

Back in the Critic-Chair I noticed myself feeling hard and cold at first (Stage 5A). I wanted to tell the Experiencer how pathetic he sounded but I also couldn't deny how difficult it has been to see his pain (Stage 5B), how terrible I feel that he has been going through that on his own, how unfair it is that I've made him feel so small and weak. I said things like "*You never should have had to hear things like that from me, I was trying to make you stronger, but I see now how much I have been weighing you down and holding you back. I would like to be more encouraging and more accepting (Stage 5B). I want you to feel confident in yourself and to know your worth. But it's a cruel world out there and I'm worried that if I'm not here to hold you accountable it'll be worse out there for you in the long run. You will never be accepted; you are different, and you will never fit in. You have to learn to survive and rise above it all (Stage 5A)*".

Back in the Experiencer-Chair I felt hurt but calmer somehow, like I couldn't expect the Critic to be any different. I also felt angry because the Critic was being completely illogical. I told him "*If I will never be accepted and I have to learn to rise above it all what good are you to me pulling me down the whole time? The odds have always been stacked against me, and I've got this far. I need you to be an ally and to support me and I'm just going to tune you out if you don't meet these terms (Stage 6A).*" I smiled to myself, and I noticed I was feeling stronger, more awake somehow. I feel like I've got more tools to recognize and respond differently to these attacks.

Box 5.2

Transforming the Self-Critic Task (Summary of Experience: Alice)

What Alice was doing during the Transforming the Self-Critic task

I thought of the time when I got upset when my son did not complete his assignment (Stage 1). In the Critic-Chair (Stage 2) I said to myself in the Experiencer-Chair: *"You are a lousy mother. You are the adult here. You should have controlled your emotions better. Even your husband is sick and tired of tolerating you and that's why he brought you to seek professional help. You are emotionally weak."* The tone was harsh and contemptuous.

In the Experiencer-Chair (Stage 3), I felt really guilty, sad, and helpless. I felt so small and worthless. I felt very hurt when hearing the Critic's criticism. It was like someone just stabbed my heart and punched me in my stomach. My heart and stomach were in pain. I needed (Stage 4) the Critic to be kinder and gentler to me. I said to the Critic: *"I need you to understand just how hard it is for me to control my emotions."*

As the Critic (Stage 5), I could see that myself in the Experiencer-Chair was going through a lot of pain, and she needed more compassion from me. I wished for her to be more emotionally resilient. It was hard for me to soften though because if I go soft with her, she would just wallow in self-pity and not learn how to better control her emotions. I said to the Self in the Experiencer-Chair: *"I will criticize you because you need to toughen up. The fact that you are so easily crushed by my criticisms just goes to show how weak and fragile you are. The world is harsh and don't expect anyone to be kind to you. I need to prepare you for what other people may do to you, so that you will not be hurt or disappointed."*

As the Self in the Experiencer-Chair, I felt hurt and lonely. I also felt angry at the Critic for being so cold and hard-hearted towards me. I said to the Critic (Stage 6A): *"I will not allow you to keep doing this to me. Just back off and give me a break. If you don't have anything nice to say to me, just don't say anything and be quiet. I know that I need to work on improving myself, but it is not okay to label me and attack my self-worth."* I felt stronger and more relieved. I feel more confident and liberated when I stood up for myself. I said to the Critic further: *"If you keep criticizing me relentlessly, I will lock you behind a door and just disregard everything you say about me."* I feel much lighter and more empowered.

Box 5.3

Summary Sheet: Transforming the Self-Critic task

Parts Enacted in the Experiencer-Chair	Parts Enacted in the Critic-Chair
	How do I criticize (attack) myself? (Increasing awareness of the way I treat myself, e.g., criticize, devalue, attack myself, etc.) _____ _____ _____ _____
	What drives my criticism? (e.g., is it a wish to improve myself? A wish to avoid interpersonal judgement and rejection? A wish to earn recognition, respect, love? Or a sense that I deserve to be punished?) _____ _____ _____ _____ _____
How do I feel when I am being treated like this (criticized, attacked, etc.)? (Reflect on the emotional impact of this which will often be variations of shame or other painful emotions.) _____ _____ _____ _____ _____	

What do I need when I'm feeling this way/in the face of criticism? (Try to articulate the need stemming from the hurt feelings directed at the critic.)

_____

_____

_____

_____

What do I feel towards the hurt, shamed, put down, vulnerable part of me? (e.g., think about bringing a reminder of the compassionate experiences that may respond to the unmet needs in the vulnerable experience accessed in the Experiencer-Chair.)

_____

_____

_____

_____

_____

How can I face the Critic? (What will help me remember that I don't have to accept what the Critic says and I can face them and stand up for myself?)

_____

_____

_____

_____

_____

Note: Remember that you do not need to undertake all the tasks at one time or in one sitting. Please feel free to attend to these tasks in your own time. You can always look up the completed examples from this chapter for Timothy and Alice in Appendix V (pages 168–170) if you need further guidance, clarification, or reference about how to undertake the task.

Quiz for Self-Assessment (See Appendix V, page 171 for Answers)

		True	False
1	We often criticize ourselves to improve and be better in our achievements or to improve how we are seen by others.	☐	☐
2	Maladaptive self-criticism can happen when we internalize problematic criticisms directed at us by our authority figures.	☐	☐
3	Self-criticism can elicit feelings of painful shame.	☐	☐
4	We can sometimes begin to actively seek out self-criticism when we start to believe we 'deserve' such self-punishment.	☐	☐
5	The Transforming the Self-Critic task is a form of the 'Self-to-Other' experiential task.	☐	☐
6	Transforming the Self-Critic task seeks to counter shame with emotional experiences such as feeling proud, loved, and appreciated.	☐	☐

Chapter 6

Transforming Interpersonal Emotional Injury (Unfinished Business)

Learning Goals

1 To bring our focus to another process that can assist us in transforming our longstanding painful feelings stemming from difficult interactions with others.
2 To enhance our understanding of the impact problematic interactions with others had on us emotionally and how it may shape our feelings in some situations now.
3 To learn an experiential task that is focused on transforming emotional injuries caused by emotionally painful interpersonal interactions or by experience of loss.

Suggested duration: One week

Introduction

Building on the learnings gained in the previous chapter, in this chapter we will focus on the second process that can assist us in transforming our longstanding painful feelings, stemming from painful interpersonal injuries into a more helpful and tolerable emotional experience. Many of our triggers of core painful feelings stem from difficult interpersonal interactions, particularly those that occurred during developmentally sensitive times such as childhood or during adolescence. When we go through repeated patterns of long-term painful experiences the resulting emotional injuries tend to become more chronic and persisting. Emotional injuries are often experienced within significant relationships (such as those with parents or important peers or other important people such as teachers, siblings, friends, romantic partners, etc.), when our interactions with another leave us feeling rejected, judged, neglected, intruded upon, undermined, scared, or experiencing a sense of being burdened. Therefore, in this chapter we will become more aware of how emotional injuries impact our emotional experience and how they can shape our emotional sensitivities (emotional vulnerabilities). We will also consider how we can process such emotional injuries so that we can meet our emotional needs.

Transforming Emotional Injury

Difficult interpersonal interactions can be generally classified as two different kinds: historical or recent. Sometimes the pain we experience is a result of the mixture of these two. For example, a problematic relationship with an important person in our

DOI: 10.4324/9781003201861-7

life that was historically problematic (e.g., a parent communicated their disappointment with us, or was not available when we needed them) and is still problematic (e.g., remains inconsistently available and critical of us in adulthood). It is important to remember that while our emotional injuries are certainly important factors in the development of chronic painful feelings, the way in which we treat ourselves in the moment (for example, with self-criticism as we saw in the previous chapter) tends to further compound the pain and injury. In the beginning the tendency to criticize ourselves may have developed with the intention of reducing the emotional pain that resulted from an emotional injury experienced in relation to a significant other. For example, we may have experienced an emotional injury from our parents and then started self-criticism to improve ourselves so that our parents may finally approve of us. However, in the long run such strategies (e.g., self-criticism) only serve to make our pain more persistent. It is therefore vital that we aim to transform such underlying emotional injuries and heal our emotional wounds.

The Transforming from Interpersonal Emotional Injury task works on experiences of interpersonal emotional injury that often have *historical* origins. For example, this may be a person like a dismissive teacher from whom you received messages like "*you are not good enough*" and towards whom you have some unresolved feelings. It may include experiences when others where not there when you needed them (e.g., a dad/mum not showing up at the football pitch during an important game). It may include experiences of traumatic fear (e.g., being physically threatened by a bully). It may also involve more *recent* experiences that were *particularly* painful (e.g., a betrayal from a friend). These types of experiences not only leave emotional scars, but they can shape how we experience future events that have some similarities to the ones that hurt us.

We develop emotional sensitivities (vulnerabilities) that may potentially colour our experiences of other interactions. The emotional vulnerability can thus become more chronic and difficult to shift. We will focus here on an experiential task which will help you to be able to (1) bear the pain contained in the emotional wound, (2) articulate the interpersonally oriented unmet needs you have when feeling the painful wound, and (3) get a compassionate and/or supportive response to this wound (and those unmet needs) or form a healthy, boundary-setting anger that allows for healing. Given such potential for growth and healing, the Transforming Interpersonal Emotional Injury task can sometimes be referred to as the Unfinished Business task.

Pre-Task Requirements: This task can be applied to a significant current or historic relationship that may still be resulting in painful feelings of loneliness, sadness, shame, and/or fear. In this task both your Self and an imagined Other would sit on different chairs. This Other person would primarily be the Injurer (i.e., person who has caused the emotional injury). However, in some circumstances, you may also be asked to imagine a caring and responsive other person who will also use the Other-Chair.

For this task you will need two chairs: The Self-Chair (i.e., your own chair) and the Other-Chair (for the imagined other person) that is placed opposite to your own chair. That is, the two chairs should be facing each other. The chair on the left will be called the Self-Chair, and the chair on the right will be called the Other-Chair. See Figure 6.1 for reference. Please be seated in the Self-Chair at the start of the task in a comfortable position and begin by focusing on your breathing.

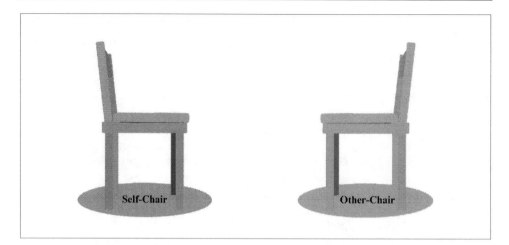

Figure 6.1 Chair positions for the Transforming Interpersonal Emotional Injury task. Self-Chair is on the left side and Other-Chair is on the right side.

Description of Main Stages of the Transforming Interpersonal Emotional Injury task

In this section we briefly explain the main steps that are involved in this task. This is helpful to prepare you for the task and provide the rationale behind it. Please note that you don't need to undertake these instructions at this time. You will be provided with detailed guidance sheets in this chapter that are designed to be used when you are ready to undertake the task. Use this section only as an educational piece to help you become familiar with what to expect in the task and use the detailed guidance sheets when you are ready to practice the task.

When to use the task: The following task for 'Transforming Interpersonal Emotional Injury' has been developed to help you when you want to consider any current or historical relational interactions that may be bringing up a lingering emotional pain in you. In this task, we will real-play a conversation between you and the Other with whom you have experienced this problematic relationship. These relationships could include romantic relationships, relationships with work colleagues, relationships with siblings, other relatives, or friends/peers. These could also be relationships with your biological parents, adoptive parents, or stepparents. These people need not be alive or in contact with you currently. It is important that you select a person with whom you have had a significant relationship but not anyone who has been actively abusive or too terrifying. In such instances, we recommend that you talk to a therapist or other mental health professional.

Number of stages: There are six main stages in the Transforming Interpersonal Emotional Injury task, as described in the following:

Stage 1 – Becoming Aware of the Emotional Hurt

In this stage you will be asked to begin thinking about a person who has caused you an emotional injury that you feel able to bring here in your imagination and try this task with. Take your time in selecting a person and please do not select anyone who has been actively abusive or too terrifying in your experience. It should be a significant Other from whom you have received painful messages in the past and towards whom you may have some unresolved feelings. We also recommend that when you try this task for the first time that you do not imagine a person with whom the interaction was too problematic. It is easier to learn this task with some 'unfinished business' that is not too upsetting. Once you learn the task you can try it with a more complex issue, but always monitor whether you feel okay enough to imagine that other person. You will then be asked to try to picture this Other sitting opposite you in the Other-Chair. Imagine that they are there in front of you and are also looking at you, as you continue to look at him or her. Then you will be guided to try and sense what happens inside you when you see the Other there opposite to you. Here you will consider what this brings up for you and what you feel.

Stage 2(A) – Expressing the Pain, Hurt, and Anger

In Stage 2(A), you will be guided to have a conversation with this Other person imagined to be sitting in the opposite Other-Chair. Remember that this is not a rehearsal for a real conversation. It is an internal conversation that should help you clarify what you are feeling and help you better understand what are the related unmet needs that these feelings may be responding to. You will then be guided to tell this imagined Other what you feel inside when you see them here (it may involve the feelings that you felt in relation to the interaction you had with them).

Stage 2(B) – Enactment of the Hurtful/Neglectful Other

In Stage 2(B), once you have expressed to the imagined Other what you feel, you will be guided to move over to the Other-Chair and be that Other who has brought up these feelings in you. In this stage, you will be guided to accurately enact the way in which the Other was with you. Here we are trying to grasp what it is that you experience as difficult in the Other's behaviour towards you. Sometimes this might be about their judgement of you, or the way in which they speak and behave towards you could be making you feel threatened or rejected, or it may be that they do not show enough interest or are unable to show it (as they themselves suffer). You will be guided to enact how the Other was and express their behaviour in the sorts of messages you perceived them giving you.

Stage 3 – Experiencing the Impact of the Other's Behaviour

In Stage 3, once you have clearly enacted the Other, you will be guided to swap chairs and become yourself again in the Self-Chair. You will then be asked to try and feel how the behaviour from the Other affects your internal experience and your feelings. Then you will express this to the Other in the opposite chair as if they were sitting right there in front of you. Remember that this is not a rehearsal for talking to the Other in real life, it is just for you to get clarity about what you feel and what you need. By expressing your emotions this way, you will be able to feel and understand them better.

Stage 4 – Expressing Unmet Needs

In Stage 4, as you express your feelings (the wound the Other's behaviour brought out in you) in the moment, you will be guided to ask yourself what you need from this Other and then be guided to tell this Other what you need from him or her at this moment in the context of the feelings you feel.

Stage 5 – Checking for the Response from the Enacted Other

Once you have been able to clearly express what you need from this Other, you will be guided to return to the Other-Chair and become that imagined Other again. Now as the Other, you will be guided to consider what feelings come to you when you see yourself (i.e., the Self on the opposite Self-Chair) feeling all that pain and hurt. At this stage, two things could happen:

1 The imagined Other enacted by you does not feel compassion coming towards yourself in the Self-Chair or has some compassion but has difficulty in expressing it: If this Other is not feeling any compassion towards the Self or has some compassion but is unable to express it, you will be guided to continue the task through Stage 5(A). **OR**
2 Alternatively, the imagined Other enacted by you feels some compassion towards you in the Self-Chair. If the Other is being understanding and experiencing some compassion, you will be guided to continue the task through Stage 5(B).

Stage 6 – Reflecting and Building Boundaries

If in the previous stage the Other did not soften or let go, you will now be asked in Stage 6(A) to sit in the Self-Chair and see whether you can put a boundary to the Other. Let them know what is not okay from your perspective and tell them what you needed from them. You will then be asked to imagine a Compassionate Other person, someone who is responsive to you and will be understanding of your pain. Here you will be guided to complete some additional steps mentioned in a variant stage, called Stage 5(B2). Then you will be asked to complete the task by moving on to Stage 6(B).

Alternatively, if in Stage 5 the Other did indeed soften, tried to let go, and expressed concern for the wounded you (the Self in the Self-Chair), you will instead be asked to directly complete Stage 6(B). However, if in Stage 5 the Other did not soften, and you were directed to first complete Stage 5(B2) where a Compassionate Other person expressed compassion towards you instead of the Other, you will now be asked to see how it feels to receive this compassionate response from the Compassionate Other.

As before, the description of this task should make a lot more sense when you've had a chance to practice the task using the guidance sheets in the next section. Please do not worry about remembering all the stages as the guidance sheets will give you clear instructions about what to do in every stage of the task. You can also review how Timothy and Alice approached this task in Boxes 6.1 and 6.2. Please remember that throughout this task, you are required to focus on your feelings and emotions, rather than on your thoughts. Remember also to take as much time as you need to complete the steps.

Important Note: For this task, it is important that you select a person with whom you have had a significant relationship but not anyone who has been actively abusive or too terrifying. Please note that the current task in this self-guided form may not be suitable for working with such intense emotionally painful experiences. Working through such difficult emotionally painful experiences may best be done alongside a trained professional.

Remember: If you feel any kind of upset due to undertaking this task, you could try undertaking the 'Compassionate Self-Soothing' task or the 'Clearing a Space' task that you have previously learned in Chapter 2.

Task Variant: Emotional Injury due to the Loss of a Caring Other

A variant of the Transforming Interpersonal Emotional Injury task is when the emotional injury represents grief about the loss of somebody with whom you had a very good relationship and whom you miss a lot. In this case, where there is only the grief of loss of a Caring Other person and there are no other unresolved issues in the relationship, you should only undertake stages 1, 2A, 3, 4, 5B, and 6B. The guidance sheets for this variant pertaining to grief or loss have also been provided in this chapter. If your aim is only to undertake this variant of the Transforming Interpersonal Emotional Injury task, that relates to grief or loss, please skip directly to the Transforming Emotional Injury: Variant Guidance Sheets on page 117.

Transforming Emotional Injury: Main Task Guidance Sheets

STAGE I

BECOMING AWARE OF THE EMOTIONAL HURT
(Seating Position: on the <u>Self-Chair</u> to the left)

--

1   As we begin, please be seated in a comfortable position, and focus on your breathing.
2   Remember to take as much time as you need to complete the following steps.
3   In this task, we will real-play a conversation between you and an imagined Other with whom you have experienced some problematic interaction. Both you and the Other will sit on different chairs. Consider the chair you are currently sitting on as the Self-Chair and the opposite chair as the Other-Chair.
4   Begin to think of a person that you feel able to bring here in your imagination and try this task with. Take your time selecting this person. This person should be someone from whom you received painful messages and towards whom you may have some unresolved feelings.

(Note: In the initial few practices of this task, please select somebody with whom the upset was manageable. Please do not select anyone who has been actively abusive or too terrifying.)

5   Try to imagine this person sitting opposite you in the Other-Chair. Imagine that this Other is actually there in front of you and is also looking at you, as you continue to look at him or her.
6   What happens inside you when you see them there? What does this bring up for you? What do you feel? Try to stay with this image of the other person and see what you are feeling inside.
     Do you feel tension, hurt, or discomfort? Are there any painful or ambivalent feelings that come to you when you see this other person in front of you?
7   When you are ready, please proceed to Stage 2(A).

STAGE 2(A)

EXPRESSING THE PAIN, HURT, AND ANGER
(Seating Position: on the <u>Self-Chair</u> to the left)

--

1   Now, you are going to have a conversation with this imagined Other person. Remember this is not a rehearsal for a real conversation – it is an internal conversation that should help you clarify what you feel and help you better understand what unmet needs these feelings are responding to.
2   Tell this other person what you feel inside when you sit here. Speak to them as if they were here, right in front of you. Try to observe what you are feeling and express it as if the other person was sitting there ready to listen.
3   Take as much time as you need to express yourself.
4   When you have completed these steps, please proceed to Stage 2(B).

STAGE 2(B)

Enactment of the Hurtful Other
(Seating Position: on the Other-Chair on the right)

--

1   Now, move over to the Other-Chair and be that imagined Other who has brought up these uncomfortable feelings in you. Without holding back, and as accurately as you can, try to enact the way in which you perceived this person (i.e., the Other) is with you.

2   We are trying to grasp what it is that you experience as painful and difficult in the Other's behaviour. Be that Other for a moment and enact the behaviours that you find difficult. It can also be an absence of some behaviour (e.g., I am never here for you).

3   Sometimes this might be about their judgement of you, or the way they speak and behave makes you feel threatened or rejected. However, it can also be a more subtle message of how unavailable they have been due to their own preoccupations or pain. Maybe they are too angry or worried to be able to see the pain they are causing you.

4   Just see what fits for this situation with this person and enact it now as if the Other person was here and was actually expressing this behaviour and these attitudes towards you. What would this Other person say to you? Use the tone and attitude they would adopt towards you.

5   Try your best to demonstrate how you have experienced this Other behaving towards you. Don't get caught up in how accurate this is, whether the Other person would dispute this representation of their behaviour or disagree with it. Just try and remember from your own memory and enact what you perceived or what you have a sense the Other was saying to you. These are your perceptions; they do not necessarily have to match what the Other would actually say. You can also embellish what you have seen in them.

6   It is important to realize that this is how you see the Other behaving towards you or in your presence. Remember to take as much time as you need to complete this step for expressing those behaviours while being that Other person.

7   When you are ready, please proceed to Stage 3.

STAGE 3

EXPERIENCING THE IMPACT OF THE PAIN
(Seating Position: on the <u>Self-Chair</u> to the left)

--

1 Now, when you feel that you have clearly enacted the imagined Other in the Other-Chair, swap chairs and become yourself again in the Self-Chair.
2 Take a breath and try to feel how the behaviour enacted by the Other here and now affects your internal experience. What happens inside when you get that message? How does it feel? What is your sense inside when you get all this from the Other person?
3 Observe what is happening in your body in response to how this Other has just been treating you. Describe this response and then express it to the Other person again as if they are sitting there right in front of you. Tell them exactly how it feels and what this brings up for you.
4 Remember, this is not a rehearsal for talking to the Other, it is just for you to get clarity on what you feel and what you need. By expressing your emotions in this way, you can feel and understand them better.
5 Take a moment to check in with yourself here and ask yourself: *"Has there been a specific time or place when I felt like this before?"*
6 Does any memory come up for you where you felt similarly hurt, dejected, or ignored?
7 If yes, think about that memory and imagine that it was happening again. What is the felt sense inside? Express the feelings you have in the memory towards the imagined Other. If the memory involved some other person, you could also express it to this other person, from your memory. It doesn't have to be the same person (i.e., the Other) you were imaging at the start of the task.
8 When you are ready, please proceed to Stage 4.

STAGE 4

EXPRESSING UNMET NEEDS
(Seating Position: on the <u>Self-Chair</u> to the left)

--

1 As you express your feelings in the moment, ask yourself what you need from this imagined Other person in this situation. What do you feel you need in the here-and-now? And then tell the Other person in your own words what it is that you need from him or her.
2 Stick with this and really try to express it in as much detail as possible (if you are finding it difficult to do so, see the next instruction): What do you need from him or her as you feel all this inside? Try to voice out loud what you feel you really need from the Other person.
3 Optional: at times it may be difficult to express the need to the person that hurt you, in that case you may also imagine to express it to somebody who would understand what you needed. In this case, you would proceed to Stage 5A and enact the problematic Other and Stage 5(B2) and enact the responsive Other.
4 When you are ready, please proceed to Stage 5.

STAGE 5

CHECKING FOR THE RESPONSE FROM THE ENACTED OTHER

(Seating Position: on the <u>Other-Chair</u> to the right)

--

1   Once you have been able to verbally express what you need from the imagined Other, please come back to the Other-Chair.
2   Now, as the Other, what feelings come to you when you see yourself (i.e., yourself on the Self-Chair) feeling all that pain and hurt? How do you (as the Other) feel towards the Self?
3   At this stage, consider whether you as the Other feel any compassion coming towards yourself in the Self-Chair. If you do not feel compassion coming, or if you feel some compassion but have difficulties expressing it, continue below with Stage 5(A).
4   Alternatively, if as the Other you feel compassion coming towards yourself in the Self-Chair, please continue the task with Stage 5(B1).

Choose the most appropriate option from Stage 5(A) or 5(B1).

5(A) No Compassion Coming or Difficulties in Expressing Compassion

1   If you are unable to feel compassion as the Injurer-Other, what stops you from being compassionate? Or if you feel some compassion, but have difficulty expressing it, just try to say what you can and then try to see what is stopping you from feeling or expressing further compassion.
2   Try and name what is stopping your compassion and express it as best as you can to yourself in the Self-Chair.
3   Tell the Self in the Self-Chair all the reasons that you are not able to feel compassion towards them.
4   Take as much time as you need to express yourself to the Self in the Self-Chair.
5   When you have completed these steps, please come back to the Self-Chair and continue with Stage 6(A).

-Go to Stage 6(A)-

5(B1) Compassion is Coming

1   Now, as the imagined Other, see how it feels for you to have compassion towards yourself in the Self-Chair.
2   What would you like to say to the Self in the Self-Chair, now that you experience compassion towards them?
3   Take your time to express these feelings to the Self in the opposite Self-Chair.
4   When you have thoroughly expressed yourself to the Self in the Self-Chair please come back to the Self-Chair and continue with Stage 6(B).

-Go to Stage 6 (B)-

STAGE 5(B2)

CHECKING FOR THE RESPONSE FROM THE OTHER
(Seating Position: on the Other-Chair on the right)

--

Note: Only attend this stage if you have been specifically asked to do so after completing Stage 6(A).

1 Now, come back over to the Other-Chair and be this caring and responsive Other person. What would be that caring person's response to you?
2 Imagine yourself to be that caring person. Become them. What would they say to you in the Self-Chair in the context of the dialogue that just happened? How do they feel towards you?
3 Take your time to consider your feelings towards the hurt Self. What do you feel for him or her? What would you do if you could go back in time to support them?
4 Now name how you are feeling towards the hurt Self and express it to the Self in the opposite Self-Chair.
5 Take as much time as you need to tell the hurt Self in the opposite chair how you feel towards them. When you are ready, please move on to Stage 6(B).

STAGE 6(A)

REFLECTING AND BUILDING BOUNDARIES
(Seating Position: on the <u>Self-Chair</u> to the left)

--

1   Now come back to the Self-Chair.
2   So, the imagined Other is unable to see your pain or is unable to fully respond to it. The Other is either completely unable to see your perspective and respond or is staying firm in the same attitude that they always have held towards you.
3   What is your response to this? Are you going to accept that from them here-and-now?
4   What is it that you need from yourself in the context of their lack of or limited responsiveness? Name it for yourself and tell the Other what you will do for yourself.
5   If it is difficult say what you would do for yourself, try to just imagine in the moment that you had the power or capacity to be able to do this thing for yourself. Imagine if there are no barriers, what is it that you would do?
6   Now clearly tell the Other your position.
7   How does it feel when you say that? How was it to be able to stand up for yourself?
8   You may have felt more confident about yourself, or felt some relief? Tell the Other how it feels.
9   Please take as much time as you need to complete this.
10 Once you have expressed yourself, please begin to imagine a Caring Other person who would be responsive to you, someone who is able to see your pain and would want to respond to you in a helpful and supportive way. For example, this may be a parent, a grandparent, a close friend, or any significant other who would be responsive to you. If in Stage 3 you remembered an experience from when you were a child, this Caring Other person can also be you as your adult self now.
11 Imagine that this Caring person is now sitting in the Other-Chair instead of the Injurer. Take your time to imagine this Caring person in front of you in the opposite Other-Chair.
12 When you are ready, please revert to Stage 5(B2).

STAGE 6(B)

LETTING IN COMPASSION
(Seating Position: on the <u>Self-Chair</u> to the left)

--

1   Now come back to the Self-Chair.
2   At this stage you would have heard either the problematic Other or a Caring Other person express some compassion towards you. There seems to be understanding coming from this Other person towards you.
3   What is it like for you to hear those compassionate words? Can you try to let them in? How does it feel inside? Sometimes it is difficult to let feelings in. If it is the case, name and express to this Other person what makes you tentative or cautious.
4   At times, we may have a sense that we do not deserve anything nice – the self-critic steps in. If this was the case, try to notice it and put your self-criticism aside and spend some time focusing on what it feels like to let this experience of compassion wash over you.
5   Now, tell this Other person how it feels for you having received that compassionate presence from them. You might feel yourself getting emotional, feeling a sense of warmth and reassurance. Whatever it is that you're feeling, try to put that in words and direct these to the Other person.
6   Now, take a moment to pause and reflect on how you feel inside. See how it feels inside and take a few deep breaths.
7   Well-done. You have now completed the task.

Transforming Emotional Injury: <u>Variant</u> Guidance Sheets

(For Emotional Injury due to Grief or Loss of a Significant Other with whom you had only or primarily positive experiences.)

STAGE I (VARIANT VERSION)

BECOMING AWARE OF THE EMOTIONAL HURT
(Seating Position: on the <u>Self-Chair</u> to the left)

--

1   As we begin, please be seated in a comfortable position, and focus on your breathing.
2   Remember to take as much time as you need to complete the following steps.
3   In this task, we will real-play a conversation between you and an imagined Significant Other whose loss in your life may have caused emotional pain to you. Both you and the Significant Other will sit on different chairs. Consider the chair you are currently sitting on as the Self-Chair and the opposite chair as the Other-Chair.
4   Begin to think of a person that you feel able to bring here in your imagination and try this task with. Take your time selecting this person. This person should be someone whose loss caused emotional pain to you.
5   Try to imagine this person sitting opposite you in the Other-Chair. Imagine that this Other is actually there in front of you and is also looking at you, as you continue to look at him or her.
6   What happens inside you when you see them there? What does this bring up for you? What do you feel? Try to stay with this image of the Other person and continue to consider how you are feeling inside.
7   When you are ready, please proceed to Stage 2(A).

STAGE 2(A) – (VARIANT VERSION)

EXPRESSING THE PAIN, HURT, AND ANGER
(Seating Position: on the <u>Self-Chair</u> to the left)

--

1 Now, you are going to have a conversation with this imagined Other person. Remember it is an internal conversation that should help you clarify what you miss about losing this Other person.
2 Tell this Other person what you feel inside when you sit here and see them there in front of you in the Other-Chair. Speak to them as if they were here, right in front of you. What would you like to say to them?
3 Try to observe what you are feeling and express it as if the Other person was sitting there ready to listen.
4 Take as much time as you need to express yourself. When you have completed these steps, please proceed to Stage 3.

STAGE 3 (VARIANT VERSION)

EXPERIENCING THE IMPACT OF THE PAIN
(Seating Position: on the <u>Self-Chair</u> to the left)

--

1 Take a breath and try to feel how the loss of the Significant Other has affected your internal experience. What happens inside when you think about their loss? How does it feel? What is your sense inside due to the absence of this Other person from your life?

2 Try and observe what is happening in your body in response to such feelings? Describe this response and then express it to the Other person again as if they are sitting there right in front of you. Tell them exactly how it feels inside for you and what their loss brings up for you. What is it you are missing by losing them?

3 Remember, this is just for you to get clarity on what you feel and what you need. By expressing your emotions in this way, you can feel and understand them better. When you are ready, please proceed to Stage 4.

STAGE 4 (VARIANT VERSION)

EXPRESSING UNMET NEEDS
(Seating Position: on the <u>Self-Chair</u> to the left)

--

1 As you express your feelings in the moment, ask yourself what you need from this imagined Significant Other person in this situation. What do you feel you need in the here-and-now? And then tell the Other person in your own words what it is that you need from him or her.
2 Stick with this and really try to express in as much detail as possible what you need from him or her as you feel all this inside. Try to voice out loud what you feel you really need from the Other person.
3 When you are ready, please proceed to Stage 5B.

STAGE 5B (VARIANT VERSION)

LOOKING FOR CONNECTION/COMPASSION
(Seating Position: on the <u>Other-Chair</u> to the right)

--

1 Now, as the imagined Other person, see how it is to see yourself missing the Other? How do you feel towards yourself sitting opposite to you in the Self-Chair?
2 What would you like to say to the Self in the Self-Chair, when you hear them say what they need and what they miss? Can you tell them what you feel towards them? What was your (as the Other) relationship with the Self? What is it you (as the enacted Other) miss from the Self? What is it that you enjoyed when you were in each other's company? What do you (as the enacted Other) wish for the Self?
3 Take your time to express these feelings to the Self in the opposite Self-Chair.
4 When you have thoroughly expressed yourself to the Self in the Self-Chair please continue with Stage 6(B).

-Go to Stage 6(B)-

STAGE 6(B) (VARIANT VERSION)

REFLECTING AND LETTING CONNECTION/ COMPASSION IN
(Seating Position: on the Self-Chair to the left)

--

1 Now come back to the Self-Chair.
2 At this stage you would have heard the Other person expressing their feelings towards you and the feelings of what they enjoyed and maybe are now missing from the times when you were in each other's company.
3 What is it like for you to hear those compassionate/connecting words? Can you try to let them in? How does it feel inside? Do you enjoy the presence of the other? Do you miss them?
4 Now, tell this Other person how it feels for you having this conversation with them. You might feel yourself getting emotional, feeling a sense of warmth and sadness of the loss. Whatever it is that you're feeling, try to put that in words and direct these to the Other person.
5 Now, take a moment to pause and reflect on how you feel inside. See how it feels inside and take a few deep breaths. What else would you want to say to the Other? Try to focus on what you miss and what you enjoyed from the time when you were in their company.
6 Well-done. You have now completed the task.

Transforming Interpersonal Emotional Injury – Summary

Remember it is good to do the Transforming Interpersonal Emotional Injury task repeatedly across different people but also repeatedly with the same person, if it was a very pivotal relationship. Hopefully, in undertaking this task, you were able to experience some shift in your emotional experience of a recent or historical emotional interpersonal injury. Remember, it might be useful to attempt the Compassionate Self-Soothing task (Chapter 2) to help you regulate any lingering distress that you may still be experiencing whenever you do the Transforming Interpersonal Emotional Injury task. Before you go, don't forget to review the Summary Sheet (Box 6.3) for this task and take some time to reflect on your experience by filling this in anytime you do the task. Also, again, remember it is good to repeat this task several times, either with the same person in mind or across several people.

This chapter focused on the final transformative task and worked towards transforming core emotional experience associated with an emotional injury. Countering emotional injuries with other positive emotional experiences such as love, pride, protective anger, and compassion aids us in transforming and transcending these core painful experiences. As discussed, emotional interpersonal injuries can result from current or historic (or even a mixture of the two) interpersonal relationships and are often significant factors in the development of chronic and lingering painful feelings in our lives. The task for transforming emotional injuries (or unfinished business) involves using an empty chair dialogue wherein our own Self undertakes an imagined dialogue with a (Significant) Other (to whom the injury relates). Many of the key emotional injuries we experience are a consequence of interpersonal rejection, judgement, feeling being intruded upon, burdened, scared, neglected. Please remember that if the experience of the injury is too painful or scary we recommend that you seek professional help from a mental health professional. Some painful experiences concerning others may also involve experiences of loss of the person with whom you had a loving relationship.

Once you are ready to proceed, please review the narrative examples of Timothy and Alice in Boxes 6.1 and 6.2, as they recount their own experiences of completing the Transforming Interpersonal Emotional Injury task. When you have reviewed the same, you can then proceed to complete the Summary Sheet provided in this section (Box 6.3) to record your own experience of this task.

Remember: If you are feeling any kind of upset due to this task you could try undertaking the Compassionate Self-Soothing task or the Clearing a Space task that you have previously learnt in Chapter 2.

Box 6.1

Transforming Interpersonal Emotional Injury Task (Summary of Experience: Timothy)

What Timothy was doing during the Transforming Interpersonal Emotional Injury task

I pictured my father sitting opposite me in the Other-Chair (Stage 1). He was looking a bit awkward and guarded. I was feeling tense and uncomfortable, I was unsure if I would be able to say the things I wanted to. Dad has for the most part been consistent in turning up at weekends, and we've had a handful of holidays over the years, but it still doesn't compare to what it was like when we lived together as a family. It feels almost formal now, like we're expected to be on our best behaviour with each other. I'm not sure if I'm more worried about offending him and pushing him farther away or telling him what I need him to hear and him just not getting it.

In the Self-Chair I told him (Stage 2A) that I feel like he gave up on me when he left and that I was a mistake to him. I explained how scared and hurt and confused I was by his decision, and how worried I was that it was my fault. I told him how it made me feel inadequate and like I was even more of an outsider than I already was. I felt hurt and angry as I said these things.

In the Other-Chair I enacted my dad as he always was with me and he said things like (Stage 2B): *"I thought that the separation was not a big deal for you and that you knew it was about my relationship with your mum and nothing to do with you"*. Enacting him I also said that he had to pursue his happiness too but did not want me to feel bad but he was just busy with his new life and making sure that he provided for his new family and that he could be financially supportive to me too.

In the Self-Chair (Stage 3) I was feeling deflated. His response made me feel like my feelings weren't justified, like he hadn't even thought about the possibility I could have experienced things this way. I started to feel heat rising through my body and I was getting angrier that he wasn't even meeting me halfway. I told him that it seemed ridiculous that I must spell this out for him, and it was hurtful to think he never wondered or worried about any of this. I told him it felt like he was ignoring and belittling my pain, making me feel stupid for opening up about it and like I shouldn't have been bothered. I told him that I needed him (Stage 4) to try and recognize the suffering his absence has put me through, and to acknowledge the impact this had on me.

In the Other-Chair I enacted Dad and he was genuinely apologetic and heartfelt (Stage 5B): *"You are right, I should have known or at least asked how you were doing more. You always seemed so confident to me, but I see now how that might have been an act"*. *"I see now that I failed you. I hate to think that you weren't able to talk to me and I need you to know how proud I am of you"*. *"The fact that we've maintained a relationship through everything, including the pandemic, has given me a false sense of confidence that I've been able to be the father you deserved. I love you and I hope you'll give me a chance to do better going forward."*

In the Self-Chair (Stage 6B) I felt a wave of relief and validation wash over me. It was like I could finally let out the breath I'd been holding in and relax into my seat. I felt a sense of calm that radiated through my body. I have been seen and I am loved by him. He was imperfect too, but he did care about me. I told him that *"it means a lot to hear you say those things, and I feel a lot closer to you now you know"*. I could feel myself get emotional at the thought of being less alone, of having one more ally in my camp. I felt a sense of calm and contentment settle over me and a hopefulness that things might just be okay.

Box 6.2

Transforming Interpersonal Emotional Injury Task (Summary of Experience: Alice)

What Alice was doing during the Transforming Interpersonal Emotional Injury task

I pictured my mother sitting opposite me in the Other-Chair (Stage 1). She was looking at me with a frown. It made me feel sad and frightened. There was a knot in my stomach and my heart felt heavy. I had a sense that my mum has always favoured my brother over me. He could do no wrong in her eyes, but everything I did was usually viewed in the worst light. She would blame and criticize me whenever my brother got upset or injured. I told imagined Mum in the Other-Chair: "*I feel hurt and rejected by you* (Stage 2A). *I feel like I don't matter to you, and you only regard my brother as your child. I tried so hard to please you and I'm never good enough for you.*"

Enacting my perceptions of Mum in the Other-Chair (in a raised voice and harsh tone, Stage 2B) I (as Mum) said: "*You are a disappointment. I have enough things on my plate, and I thought I could count on you to take care of your brother and help me out in the house. Why can't you act like an older sister and be the bigger person, even if your brother did something wrong? You should study accounting like your brother, but you are so stubborn and insisted on studying a useless degree like art. I am overwhelmed myself and worried. I need you to be helping me and ensure that I do not need to worry about your future.*"

When I came back to the Self-Chair (Stage 3) I felt ashamed, hurt, and wronged. I felt so small and insignificant, like I didn't matter. It was like a shrinking feeling in my heart that made me want to disappear. I felt very hurt, rejected, and misunderstood by her.

I had a specific memory of when I gave my mother $500 after receiving my first pay-check, thinking that it would make her happy. However, she said, "*Your brother gave me $1000 recently. You should have listened to me and studied accounting like your brother.*"

I felt angry and hurt. I felt sad that nothing I did was ever good enough for her. I said to her: "*I need you to appreciate what I do for you* (Stage 4). *I need you to love and accept me for who I am. I need you to understand and accept what I love to do instead of imposing your ideas on me. I need you to acknowledge my feelings.*"

When I came back to the Other-Chair (Stage 5A) her response (me enacting her) was: "*I feel frustrated with you. If you would just listen to me, you would be earning so much more money and be more successful in your career. Can't you see that this is for your good?*"

Back in the Self-Chair (Stage 6A) I responded: "*I need to protect my feelings from being hurt by you again. I will keep an emotional distance from you, and I will do whatever I deem fit. I will affirm myself that I turned out just fine – I am kind, responsible, and honest.*"

I felt slightly more confident and relieved. It felt good to get this off my chest.

I imagined my late grandmother responding to me when I was upset about my mum's behaviour towards me (Stage 5B). I went to the Other-Chair and enacted my grandma. She said "*I am sorry you feel so unwanted and hurt by your mother. I am proud of you. You are beautiful and precious. I care deeply for you and feel sad when I see you suffer.*"

Back in the Self-Chair (Stage 6B) I felt moved and comforted. It was a warm feeling inside. I said to her: "*Grandma, thank you for loving me so unconditionally. I feel stronger and more secure with your love.*" I felt more at peace and less pain inside.

Box 6.3

Summary Sheet: Transforming Interpersonal Emotional Injury Task

Parts Enacted in the Self-Chair	Parts Enacted in the Other-Chair
	What was hurtful in the way the Other was behaving towards me?
	What was the implied message I heard from them?
How do I feel when I am being treated like this? (Note the emotional impact of the Other's behaviour, e.g., loneliness/sadness, shame, fear.)	
What do I need when I am/was treated like this from the Other or from somebody else? (Reflect on the unmet need stemming from the hurt feelings and identify to whom this need could be expressed.)	

What do I or the Other (caring part of me or caring part of the Other) feel towards the hurt, vulnerable part of me?

_____

_____

_____

_____

How can I protect myself if I am treated in this hurtful way again? What was helpful about my current response? (Note down something that will help you remember the sense of resolve you felt during the dialogue.)

_____

_____

_____

Note: You can find the filled examples of Timothy and Alice's versions of the Summary Sheet in Appendix VI (pages 172–174).

Quiz for Self-Assessment (See Appendix VI, page 175 for Answers)

		True	False
1	Scaring, burdening, intrusion, and neglect are some of the reasons that can lead to an experience of interpersonal emotional injury.	☐	☐
2	Chronic emotional injuries can occur due to repeated or long-term problematic interactions in both current and/or historic relationships.	☐	☐
3	Emotional injuries usually refer to experiences that generate feelings of sadness only.	☐	☐
4	We can transform emotional injuries by countering them with emotional experiences of self-worrying or self-interruption.	☐	☐
5	We can transform emotional injuries by countering them with emotional experiences of love, compassion, pride, and/or anger.	☐	☐
6	Chronic emotional injuries can severely impact our current relationships by triggering problematic, difficult to process feelings.	☐	☐

Chapter 7

Summary and Conclusion

Learning Goals

1 To celebrate the completion of the course.
2 To review and summarize the key learnings from the course.
3 To consider additional EFT-based resources and a plan for the future.

Congratulations and well-done to you for all the efforts that you have put in working through this course. You have now come to the end of the workbook, and we hope that you found the course helpful in your journey to better understand and manage your emotions. This workbook focused on emotional healing as an interplay between being friendly with our emotions, being able to respond more helpfully to them, and being able to transform the chronic painful emotions when necessary. Through introducing you to various experiential tasks, the course aimed at helping you learn to better tolerate painful emotions (such as loneliness/sadness, shame, and fear) and also sought to assist you in being able to articulate your unmet needs and understand what they point to (e.g., need for closeness, acceptance, and safety). Through this, we hope that you have been better able to respond to such needs by yourself and also able to seek healthy responses from others in appropriate ways. This process is often not easy and needs frequent repetition. However, it can be very fulfilling and can mitigate the distress and pain we feel in our lives.

We began this course by learning about how our emotions act as messengers and provide us with vital information about the state of our relationships and about the unmet needs in our lives. We learned about how emotional pain presents itself (e.g., in the form of symptoms of depression, anxiety, and irritability) and how this symptom-level distress is a manifestation of the underlying experiences of chronic loneliness/sadness/loss, shame, and/or fear and their unique mixtures.

In Chapter 2, you were introduced to two helpful tasks that can help you tolerate and regulate overwhelming emotions. These tasks were the Clearing a Space task and the Compassionate Self-Soothing task. Remember that you can use these tasks whenever you feel overwhelmed by your emotions. It is most helpful to return to these tasks on a frequent basis, as this helps in improving their effectiveness in supporting you.

In Chapter 3 and Chapter 4, you were introduced to ways in which you can overcome two unhelpful ways in which we avoid our emotions (i.e., through self-interruption and through self-worrying). You may recall that Self-Interruption is a way in which we tend to stop ourselves from expressing or feeling our emotions, or avoiding situations that could bring painful emotions. Similarly, Self-Worrying is when we

DOI: 10.4324/9781003201861-8

constantly worry and scare ourselves about upcoming events or situations as a form of self-protection against the feelings those situations might cause us, which we don't want to experience. By undertaking chair dialogue with the Self-Interrupter and the Self-Worrier, you were able to feel the deep impact of the avoidance, and understand the anxieties that drive such behaviour. You were also able to experience the cost of such obstructing or controlling self-treatment and express what you really need in the face of obstruction or worrying.

In Chapter 5 and Chapter 6, you undertook two tasks that are designed to help you in the transformation of painful emotions. The first task was to have a Self-to-Self chair in dialogue with the Self-Critic. Here you learned that we often criticize ourselves to try and better ourselves in ways that will impact others or fulfil our own ideals. While this process can be adaptive, unfortunately often enough it can lead us to feel shame and other painful feelings. By engaging with the Self-Critic, you were able to clearly articulate the impact of such criticism in your life, express what you need from the Self-Critic, and establish effective boundaries with, or ways of softening, this part of yourself.

Similarly, in the second task (Chapter 6), you focused on transforming emotional injuries or unfinished business with a Significant Other person, by engaging in a Self-to-Other chair dialogue. Here you learned that many of the triggers of emotional pain that we experience often result from previous difficult interactions or experiences with others, often during our childhood period or during adolescence. Such painful experiences often leave us feeling excluded, rejected, judged, undermined, scared, or like a burden to others. By engaging with an imagined Other who has caused you an emotional injury, you clearly articulated the impact of the Other's actions or inactions and the hurt that you experienced, and also expressed what you needed from them or for yourself. You may have experienced establishing effective boundaries with this imagined Other or allowed a compassionate Other to provide you with the compassion and understanding that you needed. We also discussed variants of this task that can be used either with a caring Other or with somebody whom we lost and with whom we had a nice and connecting relationship.

It is important to remember that once you have gone through all the tasks in this workbook, it would be helpful for you to return to the ones that you found most fitting, relevant, and important to you. You can do these tasks at any point of time if you need to, and also use the regulating tasks in Chapter 2 to regulate and manage any overwhelming or distressful feelings that may come up for you. Frequent use of these tasks will be most helpful in deepening your experience of soothing and can be helpful in allowing you to befriend and transform difficult emotions more easily over time.

We wish you all the very best in your journey ahead.

Additional Resources and Information about EFT

Here are some additional resources for you to help you plan your journey with Emotion-Focused Therapy ahead. If you would like to find an EFT-trained therapist, you can check the directory of the International Society for Emotion-Focused Therapy on their website at: www.iseft.org

Remember also that you can download all the task guidance sheets that have been presented in this workbook from the Support Material (www.routledge. com/9781032063393). These can be very helpful for you in undertaking the various tasks, and act as a quick an easy reference for you. They can also be helpful to you when you don't have access to this workbook.

For psychologists and psychotherapists, the following resources can also be useful when using EFT with your clients:

Greenberg, L. S. (2015). *Emotion-focused therapy: Coaching clients through their feelings*. 2nd ed. Washington, DC: American Psychological Association. – One of the latest accounts of EFT from the major developer of the approach.

Elliott, R., & Greenberg, L. S. (2021). *Emotion-focused counselling in action*. Sage. – A therapist-in-training friendly account of EFT.

Timulak, L. (2015). *Transforming emotional pain in psychotherapy: An emotion-focused approach*. Hove, Sussex: Routledge. – The presentation of EFT to professionals without an EFT background.

Timulak, L., & Keogh, D. (2022). *Transdiagnostic emotion-focused therapy: A clinical for transforming emotional pain*. Washington, DC: American Psychological Association. – The therapist's manual for the approach presented in this workbook.

Timulak, L., & McElvaney, J. (2018). *Transforming generalized anxiety: An emotion-focused approach*. Hove, Sussex: Routledge. – The therapist's manual specifically focused on generalized anxiety.

References

Elliott, R., Watson, J. C., Goldman, R. N., & Greenberg, L. S. (2004). *Learning emotion-focused therapy: The process-experiential approach to change.* Washington, DC: American Psychological Association. doi: 10.1037/10725-000

Gendlin, E. T. (1996). *Focusing-oriented psychotherapy. A manual of the experiential method.* New York: Guilford Press.

Greenberg, L. S. (2015). *Emotion-focused therapy: Coaching clients through their feelings.* 2nd ed. Washington, DC: American Psychological Association.

Greenberg, L. S. (2017). *Emotion-focused therapy.* Revised ed. Washington, DC: American Psychological Association.

Greenberg, L. S., Rice, L. N., & Elliott, R. (1993). *Facilitating emotional change: The moment-by-moment process.* New York: Guilford Press.

Timulak, L. (2015). *Transforming emotional pain in psychotherapy: An emotion-focused approach.* Hove, Sussex: Routledge.

Timulak, L., & Keogh, D. (2022). *Transdiagnostic emotion-focused therapy: A clinical for transforming emotional pain.* Washington, DC: American Psychological Association.

Timulak, L., & McElvaney, J. (2018). *Transforming generalized anxiety: An emotion-focused approach.* Hove, Sussex: Routledge.

Appendix 1

TASK 1: UNDERSTANDING SYMPTOMATIC DISTRESS AND UNDERLYING VULNERABILITY

Considering Symptoms of Depression

An Example of Box 1.1
_____

Reflecting on Symptoms of Depression

Timothy's Example: Symptoms of Depression

Reflect on a few unpleasant or distressing emotions and the accompanying situations which trigger these emotions. These could be depression like symptoms (e.g., feeling hopelessness, helplessness, resignation, feeling down, sad about everything, irritated, and/or feeling angry). Write these in the space provided here. *For example: I felt irritated/ resigned when my partner did not pay attention to me. (Use as much space as you need.)*

Response:

I feel exhausted all the time and can't seem to get up in the morning since the pandemic.
I feel like things will never go back to how they were before I was with Rachel.
Since I broke up with Rachel, I feel like I'll never be able to meet someone I feel 100%
*   about and I'll end up on my own.*
I feel guilty that I've hurt Rachel by breaking up with her.

An Example of Box 1.1
_____

Reflecting on Symptoms of Depression

Alice's Example: Symptoms of Depression

Reflect on a few unpleasant or distressing emotions and the accompanying situations which trigger these emotions. These could be depression like symptoms (e.g., feeling hopelessness, helplessness, resignation, feeling down, sad about everything, irritated, and/or feeling angry). Write these in the space provided here. *For example: I felt irritated/ resigned when my partner did not pay attention to me. (Use as much space as you need.)*

Response:

I feel irritated with my son for not trying harder in school.
I feel helpless when nothing I do can help my son focus better.
I feel guilty for letting my bosses down because they expected me to step up and do more
*   this year, but I continued to work part-time.*
I feel resentful towards my husband for not standing up for me whenever I had
*   disagreements with his mother.*
I felt hopeless that things will not return back to normal again, given the Covid-19 situation.

An Example of Box 1.2

Reflecting on Underlying Feelings in Depression

Timothy's Example: Underlying Feelings

Our unmet emotional needs bring emotional reactions (i.e., underlying feelings [e.g., feelings of disappointment, humiliation, embarrassment, or fear]) that we may feel *before* we get depressed. What are some of the underlying emotional reactions that you experienced in important emotional situations *before* you felt depressed? Please write in the space provided. *For example: I felt sadness that my partner was not interested in what upset me. (Use as much space as you need.)*

Response:

> *I miss Rachel because it was nice to feel close with her, I felt she wanted to get to know me, I miss feeling loved by her.*
> *I started to feel I may let her down by not being ready to move on with the relationship.*
> *I felt sad and disappointed that she would never be able to understand what it's like for me.*
> *I felt terrible for breaking up with her.*

An Example of Box 1.2

Reflecting on Underlying Feelings in Depression

Alice's Example: Underlying Feelings

Our unmet emotional needs bring emotional reactions (i.e., underlying feelings [e.g., feelings of disappointment, humiliation, embarrassment, or fear]) that we may feel *before* we get depressed. What are some of the underlying emotional reactions that you experienced in important emotional situations *before* you felt depressed? Please write in the space provided. *For example: I felt sadness that my partner was not interested in what upset me. (Use as much space as you need.)*

Response:

> *I felt sad that my son does not confide in me anymore.*
> *I felt lonely when my husband did not back me up in front of his mother and our son.*
> *I felt ashamed for being a bad mother (as my son is not doing that well in school) and wife (for having arguments with my husband).*

An Example of Box 1.3

Reflecting on Unmet Needs (Depression)

Timothy's Example: Unmet Needs

Now reflect on the unmet needs you may have had in such situations (e.g., need to be close, supported, valued, protected, etc.) that were not met. Please write them here in the space provided. *For example: my need was to be comforted by my partner. (Use as much space as you need.)*

Response:

> *I miss Rachel, I miss the intimacy and connection we had.*
> *I need to feel close to Rachel. I need to feel that my partner (or people that matter to me) understand and accept me for who I am.*
> *I also need to feel that I am welcomed, that people that matter to me love me for whom I am. I deserve to be respected regardless of other prejudices.*

An Example of Box 1.3

Reflecting on Unmet Needs (Depression)

Alice's Example: Unmet Needs

Now reflect on the unmet needs you may have had in such situations (e.g., need to be close, supported, valued, protected, etc.) that were not met. Please write them here in the space provided. *For example: my need was to be comforted by my partner. (Use as much space as you need). (Use as much space as you need.)*

Response:

> *I need to protect my son.*
> *I need to be loved and valued by my husband.*
> *I need to be accepted for who I am, not for what I can offer to others.*

Considering Symptoms of Anxiety

An Example of Box 1.4

Reflecting on Symptoms of Anxiety

Timothy's Example: Symptoms of Anxiety

Try to reflect on feelings of anxiety (e.g., nervousness, tension, hypervigilance) that you may have felt in *advance* of a situation that may potentially bring painful feelings. Please write them in the space provided. *For example: I feel anxious ahead of the meeting with my line manager. (Use as much space as you need.)*

Response:

>   *As soon as I wake up and notice the time I get scared that my boss is going to be angry that I've been coming in late (nervous/anxious).*
>   *I feel like people are treating me differently in work and that I'm going to lose my job (hypervigilance).*
>   *I am anxious about contacting Rachel out of fear that she may be angry at me (or upset).*

An Example of Box 1.4

Reflecting on Symptoms of Anxiety

Alice's Example: Symptoms of Anxiety

Try to reflect on feelings of anxiety (e.g., nervousness, tension, hypervigilance) that you may have felt in *advance* of a situation that may potentially bring painful feelings. Please write them in the space provided. *For example: I feel anxious ahead of the meeting with my line manager. (Use as much space as you need.)*

Response:

>   *I feel anxious ahead of my son's school tests.*
>   *I feel tense whenever I cannot fall back asleep at night because I am worried that I cannot function the next day.*
>   *I feel anxious ahead of leaving the house because I am worried about contracting Covid-19 or a similar illness.*
>   *I am anxious that I will get criticized by my mother-in-law for how I respond to my son's progress in school.*

An Example of Box I.5

Reflecting on Underlying Feelings in Anxiety

Timothy's Example: Underlying Feelings of Anxiety
(i.e., what you were dreading)

Anxiety tells us that we are dreading some situations and are fearful of the feelings that these situations may bring. What feelings would be difficult to feel in the situations you are dreading. These may, for instance, include feelings of being rejected, feeling alone, feeling not valued, feeling unprotected, or feeling scared. Please write them in the space provided. *For example: feeling humiliated by seeming incompetent in front of my line manager. (Use as much space as you need.)*

Response:

I'm bad at my job because I've put on weight.
I'll be embarrassed if I lose my job. I would disappoint my mum and it would be unbearable.
I feel profoundly alone (without Rachel), without other close ones (Dad).
I have a sense I do not belong; I am too different from others.

An Example of Box I.5

Reflecting on Underlying Feelings in Anxiety

Alice's Example: Underlying Feelings of Anxiety
(i.e., what you were dreading)

Anxiety tells us that we are dreading some situations and are fearful of the feelings that these situations may bring. What feelings would be difficult to feel in the situations you are dreading. These may, for instance, include feelings of being rejected, feeling alone, feeling not valued, feeling unprotected, or feeling scared. Please write them in the space provided. *For example: feeling humiliated by seeming incompetent in front of my line manager. (Use as much space as you need.)*

Response:

I feel flawed as a mother for not being able to help my son cope better in school.
I feel alone at night when everyone else is asleep and I have no one to turn to.
I feel inadequate for being an imposter at work and not living up to my managerial position.
I feel fearful of dying from Covid-19 or a similar illness.

An Example of Box 1.6

Reflecting on Unmet Needs (Anxiety)

Timothy's Example: Unmet Needs

What emotional needs do these feelings point to? For instance, these may include needs such as the need to be accepted, to be safe, to be appreciated, to be cared for. Please write them in the space provided. *For example: I would want to be acknowledged by my line manager. (Use as much space as you need.)*

Response:

> *I need my work to be recognized and valued.*
> *I need to feel more appreciated and accepted for who I am outside of work.*
> *I need to feel that I matter to my dad.*
> *I need to feel loved as I felt loved by Rachel.*
> *I need to feel like I belong to a broader community.*
> *I want my mum to be proud of me.*

An Example of Box 1.6

Reflecting on Unmet Needs (Anxiety)

Alice's Example: Unmet Needs

What emotional needs do these feelings point to? For instance, these may include needs such as the need to be accepted, to be safe, to be appreciated, to be cared for. Please write them in the space provided. *For example: I would want to be acknowledged by my line manager. (Use as much space as you need.)*

Response:

> *I would want to be appreciated by my family for being a good enough mother.*
> *I would want to be supported by my husband whenever I cannot sleep.*
> *I would want to be acknowledged and valued by my bosses and other important people like my mother-in-law.*
> *I would want to be protected and to be safe.*

TASK 2: UNDERSTANDING CORE EMOTIONAL PAIN

Considering the Sadness/Loneliness Cluster

An Example of Box 1.7

Reflecting on Feelings of Sadness/Loneliness

Timothy's Example: Sadness/Loneliness Cluster (Feelings)

Now try to reflect on your own emotional vulnerabilities and sensitivities. Which of these seem to belong to the 'Sadness/Loneliness' cluster (e.g., feeling alone, missing loved ones, feeling sad, missing love or connection and similar feelings)? Please write them in the space provided. *(Use as much space as you need.)*

Response:

Growing up as the only mixed-race person in my school left me feeling lonely and isolated at times, and then when Dad left it was like it was just me and mum against the world.
Mum would work long hours and I would be at home on my own a lot.
Everyone else I knew fitted in somewhere. My mum has her family, my cousins had each other.
When I got together with Rachel it was great, it was nice to be wanted and to feel cared for. Now I feel alone again.

An Example of Box 1.7

Reflecting on Feelings of Sadness/Loneliness

Alice's Example: Sadness/Loneliness Cluster (Feelings)

Now try to reflect on your own emotional vulnerabilities and sensitivities. Which of these seem to belong to the 'Sadness/Loneliness' cluster (e.g., feeling alone, missing loved ones, feeling sad, missing love or connection and similar feelings)? Please write them in the space provided. *(Use as much space as you need.)*

Response:

Feeling alone in my marriage.
Missing the connection and close bond I used to share with my son when he was younger.
Feeling sad that I never received the approval and love from my parents.
Feeling isolated from my friends.
Feeling empty, like my life has no meaning.

An Example of Box 1.8

Reflecting on Unmet Needs in Sadness and Loneliness

Timothy's Example: Sadness/Loneliness Cluster (Unmet Emotional Needs)

Now please try to reflect on the corresponding emotional needs (e.g., longing for connection, love, closeness, and so on) that those emotions may be connected to. Please write them in the space provided. *(Use as much space as you need.)*

Response:

I want to feel less alone, to be close to others and for that to come easily.
I want to feel like I belong (I have that in the gym).
I miss the connection with my dad.
I miss Rachel.
I miss spending more time with my mum.

An Example of Box 1.8

Reflecting on Unmet Needs in Sadness and Loneliness

Alice's Example: Sadness/Loneliness Cluster (Unmet Emotional Needs)

Now please try to reflect on the corresponding emotional needs (e.g., longing for connection, love, closeness, and so on) that those emotions may be connected to. Please write them in the space provided. *(Use as much space as you need.)*

Response:

I long for a deeper connection and closeness with my husband.
I long for a deeper connection and closeness with my parents.
I long for closeness and care from my friends.

Considering the Shame Cluster

An Example of Box 1.9

Reflecting on Feelings of Shame

Timothy's Example: Shame Cluster (Feelings)

The Shame cluster includes experiences of feeling humiliated, embarrassed, inadequate, flawed, worthless, and similar feelings. Do you recognize any of such feelings in your own experience when you experienced difficult situations? If yes, please write them in the space provided. *(Use as much space as you need.)*

Response:

I felt really different in school. People never let me forget that I looked different.
I feel I am not clever enough; it is too hard when the letters and words get jumbled on my page.
When Dad left, I felt so ashamed, like our family was too different.
I felt like he had seen through me and knew I wasn't good enough for him.
I feel like I do not deserve Rachel.

An Example of Box 1.9

Reflecting on Feelings of Shame

Alice's Example: Shame Cluster (Feelings)

The Shame cluster includes experiences of feeling humiliated, embarrassed, inadequate, flawed, worthless, and similar feelings. Do you recognize any of such feelings in your own experience when you experienced difficult situations? If yes, please write them in the space provided. *(Use as much space as you need.)*

Response:

I feel inadequate as a mother, wife, daughter, and daughter-in-law.
I feel worthless as I do not feel particularly wanted by my parents.
I feel like a useless mother as my son is not doing that well academically.
I feel embarrassed for being weak.
I feel like I am letting down my co-workers for not working full-time.

An Example of Box 1.10

Reflecting on Unmet Needs in Shame

Timothy's Example: Shame Cluster (Unmet Emotional Needs)

Now, as before, please try to reflect on the corresponding emotional needs (e.g., such as being accepted, valued, recognized, and so on) related to the Shame feeling. Please write them in the space provided. *(Use as much space as you need.)*

Response:

I want to be accepted for who I am by people who matter to me.
I want to feel loved for who I am by my dad.
I want to know that Rachel liked me as a person.
I want to be valued in my work.
I want people to understand how it is to be different.
I want people to understand that I did not choose to have dyslexia.
I think I need to feel better understood and valued by both my parents for how hard things have been for me growing up. I think I probably need to be more understanding and caring from myself as well.

An Example of Box 1.10

Reflecting on Unmet Needs in Shame

Alice's Example: Shame Cluster (Unmet Emotional Needs)

Now, as before, please try to reflect on the corresponding emotional needs (e.g., such as being accepted, valued, recognized, and so on) related to the Shame feeling. Please write them in the space provided. *(Use as much space as you need.)*

Response:

I need my emotions to be acknowledged and accepted by people who matter to me.
I need to be valued and appreciated by my colleagues.
I need to be loved and accepted as good enough by my parents.
I need to be accepted for who I am, no matter what I do, by my husband and people that matter to me.

Considering the Fear Cluster

An Example of Box 1.11

Reflecting on Feelings of Fear

Timothy's Example: Fear Cluster (Feelings)

The Fear cluster consists of experiences of being scared, unprotected, terrified, and such related feelings. If you can recognize some of these feelings that you may have experienced in a difficult situation in your own life, please write them here in the space provided. *(Use as much space as you need.)*

Response:

> *If I'm being really honest, I'm terrified I'm going to end up alone and unsupported in facing what life will bring me.*

An Example of Box 1.11

Reflecting on Feelings of Fear

Alice's Example: Fear Cluster (Feelings)

The Fear cluster consists of experiences of being scared, unprotected, terrified, and such related feelings. If you can recognize some of these feelings that you may have experienced in a difficult situation in your own life, please write them here in the space provided. *(Use as much space as you need.)*

Response:

> *I am fearful of the pain from dying of Covid-19.*
> *I am terrified of losing my husband and son if anything bad were to happen to them.*
> *I am scared of being left alone and unsupported in life.*

An Example of Box 1.12

Reflecting on Unmet Needs in Fear

Timothy's Example: Fear Cluster (Unmet Emotional Needs)

Now please try to write the corresponding emotional needs (such as being safe, protected, and so on) that relate to the Fear feelings. Please write them in the space provided. *(Use as much space as you need.)*

Response:

> *I need to feel secure and supported.*
> *I want to feel like I am belonging and that others have my back.*

An Example of Box 1.12

Reflecting on Unmet Needs in Fear

Alice's Example: Fear Cluster (Unmet Emotional Needs)

Now please try to write the corresponding emotional needs (such as being safe, protected, and so on) that relate to the Fear feelings. Please write them in the space provided. *(Use as much space as you need.)*

Response:

> *I need to be safe.*
> *I need to be supported by others.*
> *I need to be taken care of by others.*

TASK 3: TRIGGERS OF EMOTIONAL PAIN

An Example of Box 1.13

Reflecting on Recent Triggers of Emotional Pain

Timothy's Example: Emotional Triggers (Recent)

Try to reflect on a *recent* emotionally charged situation in your life. What triggers did you encounter? *For example: loss, exclusion, rejection, danger.* Please write them in the space provided. *(Use as much space as you need.)*

Response:

I was working with a regular client in the gym the other day, but they were much quieter than usual. They didn't book another session at the end like they usually do.
Rachel did not check in with me for some time now, I am not sure whether I matter to her at all.
When I do not hear form my dad for a week or two, I feel like I do not matter to him.
Colleagues from the gym went out and did not invite me.

An Example of Box 1.13

Reflecting on Recent Triggers of Emotional Pain

Alice's Example: Emotional Triggers (Recent)

Try to reflect on a *recent* emotionally charged situation in your life. What triggers did you encounter? *For example: loss, exclusion, rejection, danger.* Please write them in the space provided. *(Use as much space as you need.)*

Response:

I was asking my son how his day at school was, but he ignored me and was preoccupied with his computer games. I raised my voice and proceeded to turn off his computer after he told me to leave him alone. He then told me that he hated me.
My mother-in-law saw it and I am sure she was talking about it to my husband.
My boss stopped asking me whether I would go to work full-time.
My husband forgot about my birthday.

An Example of Box 1.14

Reflecting on Past Triggers of Emotional Pain

Timothy's Example: Emotional Triggers (Lifespan)

Now, please take a few moments to write down examples of the important triggers that you have felt shaped or affected by throughout the course of your life (e.g., loss, exclusion, rejection, danger). Such an exploration can often help in aiding us to become more aware of our personal emotional vulnerabilities. Please write them in the space provided. *(Use as much space as you need.)*

Response:

> *Being teased in primary school for not doing well at the weekly spelling tests.*
> *Mum and Dad had brought me to my favourite restaurant as a treat and then in the car on the way home they told me Dad was moving away. I didn't understand why or for how long but I didn't know how to say any of that.*
> *Shooting the winning basket at a basketball game in school and the other team tried to argue it wasn't fair because I clearly wasn't from the school and had just been "imported to play" against them.*
> *Going to visit my cousins with Mum and not being able to understand their in-jokes and slang words. Being referred to as their 'White' cousin.*
> *Meeting Rachel's friends for the first time and them asking me where I was from. Rachel didn't seem to understand how annoyed this made me.*
> *Meeting Dad's girlfriend for the first time and seeing how at ease and relaxed they were with each other. Knowing he was happy without us.*

An Example of Box 1.14

Reflecting on Past Triggers of Emotional Pain

Alice's Example: Emotional Triggers (Lifespan)

Now, please take a few moments to write down examples of the important triggers that you have felt shaped or affected by throughout the course of your life (e.g., loss, exclusion, rejection, danger). Such an exploration can often help in aiding us to become more aware of our personal emotional vulnerabilities. Please write them in the space provided. *(Use as much space as you need.)*

Response:

> *In kindergarten, I made a Mother's Day card for my mother, but I found it in the trash bin the next day.*
> *In primary school, I scored 80 marks in a science test, my mother said I should work harder and aim for 90 the next time.*
> *I had an argument with my brother as he messed up my artwork and he started crying. My mother shouted at me without finding out what happened.*
> *My first boyfriend of two years broke up with me because he said I was too needy, and he was too tired of my emotions.*
> *My son had an accident in the playground when he was 3 and my mother-in-law scolded me for not watching him closely.*

An Example of Box 1.15

Reflecting on Triggers of Emotional Pain and Corresponding Underlying Emotions

Timothy's Example: Emotional Triggers and Underlying Emotions (Lifespan)

Take a few moments to identify what underlying emotions (as opposed to symptoms of distress) were triggered by the experiences you reflected on in the last task. Often such emotions include variants of experiences of loss, sadness, shame, and fear. Please write them in the space provided. *(Use as much space as you need.)*

Response:

> *I felt rejected by the class and ashamed for always doing badly.*
> *I felt sad and scared I wouldn't see my dad anymore. I was worried it was my fault and confused about what I had done to make him want to go.*
> *I was angry the team were trying to make excuses and disappointed that it was my fault somehow just for looking the way I did.*
> *I felt excluded and lonely; being so different from the people who were meant to be my family left me feeling isolated and inadequate.*
> *I felt sad that Rachel couldn't appreciate how irritating it was for me that her friends assumed I wasn't local because of how I looked.*
> *I felt excluded and like I had lost the dad I knew. I wondered if he had ever been as happy with me and Mum, if what we'd had was real at all or just a big mistake.*

An Example of Box 1.15

Reflecting on Triggers of Emotional Pain and Corresponding Underlying Emotions

Alice's Example: Emotional Triggers and Underlying Emotions (Lifespan)

Take a few moments to identify what underlying emotions (as opposed to symptoms of distress) were triggered by the experiences you reflected on in the last task. Often such emotions include variants of experiences of loss, sadness, shame, and fear. Please write them in the space provided. *(Use as much space as you need.)*

Response:

> *I felt rejected and unappreciated by my mother when she threw away the card I made for her.*
> *I felt inadequate for never being good enough for my mother.*
> *I felt rejected and unloved when my mother shouted at me, even though my brother was at fault.*
> *I felt excluded and lonely when my classmates teased me.*
> *I felt flawed and unwanted when my first boyfriend broke up with me.*
> *I felt worthless as a mother when my son had an accident.*

TASK 4: EMOTIONAL AND BEHAVIOURAL AVOIDANCE

Considering Worrying

An Example of Box 1.16

Reflecting on Worrying

Timothy's Example: Enacting the Worrying

What are the situations you would typically worry about or were worried about recently (e.g., talking to your manager)? Please write them here in the space provided. *(Use as much space as you need.)*

Response:

> *I worry that my weight gain is going to get out of control.*
> *I worry about clients and colleagues judging me for this.*
> *I'm worried I'm going to lose my job if I can't get on top of how I'm feeling.*
> *I'm worried that if I lose my job, I'll have to move home with Mum and that would disappoint her.*
> *I'm worried about being alone again and never being able to feel open and secure in a relationship.*
> *I worry that I've let Rachel down and that she hates me now.*
> *I am worried that my dad is not thinking about me.*

An Example of Box 1.16

Reflecting on Worrying

Alice's Example: Enacting the Worrying

What are the situations you would typically worry about or were worried about recently (e.g., talking to your manager)? Please write them here in the space provided. *(Use as much space as you need.)*

Response:

> *I am worried about my son slipping further behind in school.*
> *I am worried that my son's future will be ruined.*
> *I am worried that my husband will eventually abandon me.*
> *I am worried that my colleagues are talking badly about me behind my back because I have been underperforming at work.*
> *I am worried about my personal and family members' health as one of us may fall seriously ill or die from Covid-19.*
> *I am worried that my mother-in-law is really disappointed in her son's choice to marry me.*
> *I am worried that my friends will leave me because I am a lousy friend.*

An Example of Box 1.17

Reflecting on the Impact of Worrying

Timothy's Example: Impact of Worrying

How does such worrying make me feel (e.g., anxious)? Please write in the space provided. *(Use as much space as you need.)*

Response:

> *When I worry, I start to feel my heart race and my face flush, sometimes my hands get*
> *sweaty and I start to feel self-conscious about everything.*
> *At work it's really distracting, and I might lose track of something I'm trying to say.*
> *At home I get so exhausted after a while that all I want to do is switch off and watch*
> *telly and eat nice food.*

An Example of Box 1.17

Reflecting on the Impact of Worrying

Alice's Example: Impact of Worrying

How does such worrying make me feel (e.g., anxious)? Please write in the space provided. *(Use as much space as you need.)*

Response:

> *Worrying makes me feel anxious, terrified, powerless, and helpless.*
> *I feel nauseous, irritable, and panicky.*

An Example of Box 1.18

Reflecting on Worrying and Avoided Underlying Emotions

Timothy's Example: Avoided Underlying Emotions

When worrying about such situations, what are the emotions that you want to prevent yourself from feeling? What are the emotions that you were worried the situation would stir up in you (e.g., *"feeling ashamed if my line manager criticised me"*)? Please write here in the space provided the emotions that fit the situation you were worried about. *(Use as much space as you need.)*

Response:

> *I guess when I'm worrying, I'm trying not to feel shame about the possibility of losing my job and disappointing myself and my mum.*
> *When I am worrying about my future relationships, I really do not want to feel the loneliness and the sense of not belonging that I am dreading.*
> *When I worry whether I matter to others (like my dad), I really do not want to feel that I am overlooked and forgotten.*
> *When I worry, how will I put up with life? I really do not want to feel the fear of being on my own.*

An Example of Box 1.18

Reflecting on Worrying and Avoided Underlying Emotions

Alice's Example: Avoided Underlying Emotions

When worrying about such situations, what are the emotions that you want to prevent yourself from feeling? What are the emotions that you were worried the situation would stir up in you (e.g., *"feeling ashamed if my line manager criticised me"*)? Please write here in the space provided, the emotions that fit the situation you were worried about. *(Use as much space as you need.)*

Response:

> *Feeling worthless as a mother.*
> *Feeling lonely and unloved by my son, husband, parents, and unliked by my close friends.*
> *Feeling unprotected in the world with scary diseases.*
> *Feeling of not being good at my work.*

An Example of Box 1.19

Reflecting on Worrying and Avoided Behaviour

Timothy's Example: Avoided Behaviour

Has your worrying also ever led you to avoid a situation? If yes, please write in the space provided about the situation(s) which you avoided, based on your earlier experience of worrying about it. *(Use as much space as you need.)*

Response:

I used to be the first to volunteer to take on new classes in the gym or work a couple of hours behind the front desk if the admin team needed back up but now I can't face the awkwardness of making small talk or trying out a new routine. I've stopped talking to friends and to my mum as frequently as I would usually and I'm avoiding bumping into my flatmates around the house. I haven't been on a night out in months.

An Example of Box 1.19

Reflecting on Worrying and Avoided Behaviour

Alice's Example: Avoided Behaviour

Has your worrying also ever led you to avoid a situation? If yes, please write in the space provided about the situation(s) which you avoided, based on your earlier experience of worrying about it. *(Use as much space as you need.)*

Response:

I avoided initiating intimacy with my husband.
I avoided reaching out to my friends for support and companionship.
I avoided hanging out with my colleagues over lunch.
I avoided taking on major projects with higher expectations at work.
I avoided going to yoga or shopping malls.

Considering Self-Interruption

An Example of Box 1.20

Reflecting on Interruption of Emotions

Timothy's Example: Interruption of Emotions (Self-Interruption)

Can you reflect on a time when you stopped yourself from feeling a particular emotion (such as getting angry or feeling sad)? Please write about your experience(s) of self-interruption (stopping your emotions) here in the space provided. How did you stop yourself from feeling or expressing your emotions (e.g., deflecting from feeling, distracting yourself, tightening up, drinking alcohol)? *(Use as much space as you need.)*

Response:

> *When my friends or parents do ask me how I'm getting on I find myself joking about looking forward to being single again or making light of how stressed I feel about work.*
> *It's much easier to stick on a movie and order take away food than to stay with my feelings.*
> *I am trying to keep myself busy in the gym (when I am not staying in bed and trying to avoid everybody).*
> *I am trying not to look at my social media to ensure that there would not be anything that would upset me.*

An Example of Box 1.20

Reflecting on Interruption of Emotions

Alice's Example: Interruption of Emotions (Self-Interruption)

Can you reflect on a time when you stopped yourself from feeling a particular emotion (such as getting angry or feeling sad)? Please write about your experience(s) of self-interruption (stopping your emotions) here in the space provided. How did you stop yourself from feeling or expressing your emotions (e.g., deflecting from feeling, distracting yourself, tightening up, drinking alcohol)? *(Use as much space as you need.)*

Response:

> *I felt sad and lonely but stopped myself by feeling angry at myself. I would tell myself that I should not be so self-absorbed and play the self-pity card as there are many people in this world who went through worse things than me. I would also distract myself by keeping myself busy all the time with household chores and planning my family's schedule.*

An Example of Box 1.21

Reflecting on the Impact of the Interruption of Emotions

Timothy's Example: Impact of Self-Interruption

What has been the impact of stopping/interrupting yourself from feeling things in your life? Please write about it here in the space provided. *(Use as much space as you need.)*

Response:

Nobody in my life really knows how bad I feel.
Distracting myself with food and TV feels even more isolating.
It also means I'm not keeping myself as fit as I usually would.
When I succeed at keeping myself busy in the gym, I do not focus on people around me
    so I feel tired and alone.

An Example of Box 1.21

Reflecting on the Impact of the Interruption of Emotions

Alice's Example: Impact of Self-Interruption

What has been the impact of stopping/interrupting yourself from feeling things in your life? Please write about it here in the space provided. *(Use as much space as you need.)*

Response:

I end up feeling really exhausted.
I also often feel misunderstood by my loved ones.
My needs for love and acceptance are unmet.

TASK 5: PROBLEMATIC SELF-RELATING (HOW WE TREAT OURSELVES WITH SELF-CRITICISM)

An Example of Box 1.22

Reflecting on Own Self-Criticism

Timothy's Example: Criticizing the Self

Do you judge yourself? If so, how do you criticize yourself? Please write it here in the space provided. *(Use as much space as you need.)*

   Note: Try to focus on the manner of judgement of yourself as a person *(for instance, "I am a fool, I am too weak, I am not smart enough, I am inadequate, I am not looking good enough …").*

Response:

> *I'm such a slob, I've gone another day without training I'm going to end up losing this job.*
> *I am not good enough to be a personal trainer when I look this way.*
> *I'm pathetic for not being able to be more open with Rachel about why I didn't feel ready to move in with her.*
> *I'm being so stupid; I'm failing at everything I'm doing and nobody is ever going to love and accept me for who I am.*

An Example of Box 1.22

Reflecting on Own Self-Criticism

Alice's Example: Criticizing the Self

Do you judge yourself? If so, how do you criticize yourself? Please write it here in the space provided. *(Use as much space as you need.)*

   Note: Try to focus on the manner of judgement of yourself as a person *(for instance, "I am a fool, I am too weak, I am not smart enough, I am inadequate, I am not looking good enough …").*

Response:

> *I am an incompetent mother.*
> *I am too weak and that is why I succumb easily to stress.*
> *I am self-absorbed and that is why my friends shun me.*
> *I am not capable enough and that is why I cannot juggle work and my home affairs.*

An Example of Box 1.23

Reflecting on the Impact of Self-Criticism

Timothy's Example: Noticing the Impact of Judgement

Now try to notice what happens inside you when you criticize yourself like this (often we tend to feel small, worthless, inadequate, flawed, unlovable, not good enough…). Please write here, in the space provided, any feelings (or physical sensations) that you notice as you criticize yourself (*e.g., "I feel unlovable"*). (*Use as much space as you need.*)

Response:

I can feel a tightness across my chest and it's almost as if a lead weight just landed on my stomach.
I feel small and worthless like nothing I can do is good enough and there's no point trying.

An Example of Box 1.23

Reflecting on the Impact of Self-Criticism

Alice's Example: Noticing the Impact of Judgement

Now try to notice what happens inside you when you criticize yourself like this (often we tend to feel small, worthless, inadequate, flawed, unlovable, not good enough…). Please write here, in the space provided, any feelings (or physical sensations) that you notice as you criticize yourself (*e.g., "I feel unlovable"*). (*Use as much space as you need.*)

Response:

I feel inadequate as a mother, wife, daughter, and daughter-in-law.
I feel worthless, like my existence does not matter.
I feel hopeless as no matter how hard I try, nothing will ever change.

TASK 6: INTERPERSONAL EMOTIONAL INJURIES

Considering Emotional Injuries

An Example of Box 1.24

Reflecting on Own Emotional Injuries

Timothy's Example: Emotional Injuries

Reflect on some past (or recent, ongoing) interpersonal situations (e.g., where a [significant] person in your life was critical of you, threatened you, disapproved of you, was unavailable, or did not have capacity [felt too vulnerable] to be with you) that brought emotional pain to you. You can start with an example that is not that painful. Please describe the situation, the behaviour of the other, and the message you received from such behaviour in the space provided. *(Use as much space as you need.)*

Response:

> *I remember when I was growing up and I was playing for a football team that my dad almost never showed up as he was busy at work. Everybody on the team had somebody there and I was often alone, or maybe it was just my mum there, but other guys had their dads there.*
> *I felt like I wasn't important enough for him to come.*

An Example of Box 1.24

Reflecting on Own Emotional Injuries

Alice's Example: Emotional Injuries

Reflect on some past (or recent, ongoing) interpersonal situations (e.g., where a [significant] person in your life was critical of you, threatened you, disapproved of you, was unavailable, or did not have capacity [felt too vulnerable] to be with you) that brought emotional pain to you. You can start with an example that is not that painful. Please describe the situation, the behaviour of the other, and the message you received from such behaviour in the space provided. *(Use as much space as you need.)*

Response:

> *I was talking to my husband, but he was distracted by his phone. I told him he needed to be a better role model for our son who perhaps is starting to develop a phone addiction. He argued that he was in the middle of dealing with work matters but I distracted him.*
> *Our argument escalated and he said he felt suffocated and walked out of the house to have drinks with his friend. The message I received from him is he feels suffocated by me and he is rejecting me for who I am.*

An Example of Box 1.25

Reflecting on the Impact of Emotional Injuries

Timothy's Example: Emotional Injuries (Checking for Pain)

Now check inside, do you experience any sense of lingering hurt from the situation you just described? What are the lingering feelings that you may have, that are connected to these painful situations and interactions? Please list them in the space provided. *(Use as much space as you need.)*

Response:

It was just an utter sense of disappointment and sadness. I can feel it even now, and the shame that I was different, on the team, and also not having my dad there.

An Example of Box 1.25

Reflecting on the Impact of Emotional Injuries

Alice's Example: Emotional Injuries (Checking for Pain)

Now check inside, do you experience any sense of lingering hurt from the situation you just described? What are the lingering feelings that you may have, that are connected to these painful situations and interactions? Please list them in the space provided. *(Use as much space as you need.)*

Response:

I am still impacted by the argument. There is a pain in my chest when I remember the argument. It's like someone just cut a hole in my heart.
I feel hurt, lonely, and abandoned.

Answers to the Quiz for Self-Assessment for Chapter I

		True	False
1	Emotions provide us with information about how well we are getting on in our relationships.	☑	☐
2	Depression is a form of Symptomatic Distress.	☑	☐
3	Anxiety is a possible symptom of emotional pain.	☑	☐
4	Love and Connection are antidotes to experiences of loneliness, chronic sadness, and loss.	☑	☐
5	Unmet emotional needs may include our need to feel connected, to feel valued, and to feel safe.	☑	☐
6	Self-Worrying is a problematic way of responding to emotions.	☑	☐

Appendix II

An Example of Box 2.6

Summary Sheet: Compassionate Self-Soothing Task

Timothy's Example: Summary of the Compassionate Self-Soothing Task

Parts Enacted in the Self-Chair	*Parts Enacted in the Compassionate-Other-Chair*
This is what I feel when I am distressed: **Response:** *I feel like I'm failing at work and I'm going to be fired any minute.*	
	This is how the caring/compassionate person that would understand my distress would be with me: **Response:** *When I enacted my best friend, he was curious and caring. He shared his own experiences and reassured me that I'll get through what's going on. After listening he suggested some practical things to do.*
	This is how I felt towards myself when I enacted that caring Other person: **Response:** *He (me enacting him) felt caring and offering comfort.*
This is how it felt to receive their caring presence: **Response:** *I felt like my fears were acknowledged and accepted and that they understood why this was so distressing for me. I felt cared for, less alone, and calmed.*	

An Example of Box 2.6

Summary Sheet: Compassionate Self-Soothing Task

Alice's Example: Summary of the Compassionate Self-Soothing Task

Parts Enacted in the Self-Chair	Parts Enacted in the Compassionate-Other-Chair
This is what I feel when I am distressed: **Response:** *I felt guilty for raising my voice at my husband in front of my son and it was very upsetting.*	
	This is how the caring/compassionate person that would understand my distress would be with me: **Response:** *When I enacted my grandmother she was saying:"I still love you, even when you are angry. I know you get angry because you love others so deeply."*
	This is how I felt towards myself when I enacted that caring Other person: **Response:** *(Me as grandmother) I feel a lot of love, warmth, and concern.*
This is how it felt to receive their caring presence: **Response:** *I felt loved, understood, and accepted. My heart felt warm and it was like a heavy weight had been lifted.*	

Answers to the Quiz for Self-Assessment for Chapter 2

Clearing a Space task

		True	False
1	Clearing a Space task should be used when you are feeling overwhelmed.	☑	☐
2	There are four stages involved in the Clearing a Space task.	☐	☑
3	Stage 1 of the Clearing a Space task requires you to pay attention to the middle part of the body.	☑	☐
4	Stage 2 of the Clearing a Space task requires you to imagine the uncomfortable feeling disappearing from your body.	☐	☑
5	Sometimes there might be a reluctance to put some of the feelings aside. This is because the feelings need to be put aside permanently.	☐	☑
6	The Clearing a Space task should be repeated as many times as required to deepen the sense of relief.	☑	☐

Compassionate Self-Soothing task

		True	False
1	The Compassionate Self-Soothing task should be used when you want to focus on your level of emotional vulnerability.	☐	☑
2	The Compassionate Self-Soothing task has been designed to help you in regulating distress.	☑	☐
3	Unlike the Clearing a Space task, the Compassionate Self-Soothing task should not be practiced when you are feeling upset.	☐	☑
4	The Compassionate Self-Soothing task can be used at any time you are feeling distressed and want to experience some relief.	☑	☐

Appendix III

An Example of Box 3.3

Summary Sheet: Overcoming Emotional Avoidance (The Self-Interrupter)

Timothy's Example: Summary of the Overcoming Self-Interruption Task

Parts Enacted in the Experiencer-Chair	Parts Enacted in the Interrupter-Chair
	How do I stop myself from feeling? (Increasing awareness about the ways in which I interrupt myself) **Response:** *Make light of the situation, laugh it off, fill myself with food, and distract myself with TV, social media, or video games.*
	What drives my efforts to stop my feelings? What are my underlying fears that drive those efforts? **Response:** *I'm afraid that if people see my pain and do nothing about it I will truly be alone.*
What impact does the interruption have? What is the personal cost of interruption to me? **Response:** *I don't let anybody see or understand my pain, I'm replacing the emotional pain with guilt about food and these behaviours are just making me more tired and less confident each day.*	
What do I need in the face of the interruption? (Articulate the need for the interruption) **Response:** *I need to be able to feel my emotions so that they can be acknowledged and understood by others so that I know I am not on my own with them.*	
	What do I feel towards the impacted part of me? What reminders of compassionate experiences can help me let go of the interrupting process? **Response:** *I feel warmth and kindness towards that part of me that is scared and in pain. I know that I have survived really difficult experiences growing up and that I deserve to feel close and connected to others. I work hard and I care about what I do, I am trying to understand myself better and help meet the needs that have gone overlooked by others in my life.*

How can I face the interruption? What points can help me remember how I faced the Interrupter in this task and allowed myself to express my emotions?
Response: *My emotions are affecting me whether I choose to face them or not. I want to learn how to be informed by my emotions instead of running away from them.*

An Example of Box 3.3

Summary Sheet: Overcoming Emotional Avoidance (The Self-Interrupter)

Alice's Example: Summary of the Overcoming Self-Interruption Task

Parts Enacted in the Experiencer-Chair	Parts Enacted in the Interrupter-Chair
	How do I stop myself from feeling? (Increasing awareness about the ways in which I interrupt myself) **Response:** *Saying to myself: "It's pointless to feel because she doesn't care, and you will be hurt even more for being too needy." Distract yourself by watching movies; control your breath; tilt your head up to hold back your tears; and numb your heart.*
	What drives my efforts to stop my feelings? What are my underlying fears that drive those efforts? **Response:** *Fear of rejection by mother-in-law.*
What impact does the interruption have? What is the personal cost of interruption to me? **Response:** *Feeling helpless and suffocated.*	
What do I need in the face of the interruption? (Articulate the need for the interruption) **Response:** *Need to be free to feel what I feel; need to be validated and accepted.*	
	What do I feel towards the impacted part of me? What reminders of compassionate experiences can help me let go of the interrupting process? **Response:** *I feel caring towards the impacted part of me. Reminding myself of my dog licking me and loving me no matter what I do.*
How can I face the interruption? What points can help me remember how I faced the Interrupter in this task and allowed myself to express my emotions? **Response:** *I am already suffering from my emotions and the Interrupter is making the pain worse. I need to be comforted, instead of being silenced for how I feel. If the Interrupter is unable to comfort me, I will comfort myself by imagining my dog showing unconditional love to me.*	

Answers to the Quiz for Self-Assessment for Chapter 3

		True	False
1	Interruption of emotions helps us avoid our feared emotional experiences but can cause us to feel constricted and unexpressed.	☑	☐
2	Some of the ways in which we avoid our emotions include using strategies such as distraction, worrying, and use of substances.	☑	☐
3	The Overcoming Self-Interruption task is useful to undertake when you are feeling afraid of expressing some of your feelings.	☑	☐
4	The Overcoming Self-Interruption task is useful to undertake when you catch yourself wanting to avoid your feelings.	☑	☐
5	The Overcoming Self-Interruption task is a useful way to overcome Self-Criticism.	☐	☑
6	If feeling distressed after doing the Overcoming Self-Interruption task, it may be helpful to undertake the Clearing a Space task.	☑	☐

Appendix IV

An Example of Box 4.3

Summary Sheet: Overcoming Worrying (The Self-Worrier)

Timothy's Example: Summary of the Overcoming the Self-Worrier Task

Parts Enacted in the Experiencer-Chair	Parts Enacted in the Worrier-Chair
	How do I worry myself? (Increasing awareness of the ways you worry yourself): **Response:** *I remind myself of all the worst-case scenarios about being judged by others, being found out as a failure, and losing any sense of identity, acceptance or belonging I have fought so hard to gain.*
	What drives my worries? (Try to focus on the underlying fears that worrying tries to prevent to be fulfilled) **Response:** *Fears of being rejected and excluded, of ending up alone.*
What impact does the worrying have? What is the emotional, physical, and personal cost to me? **Response:** *It's exhausting and distracting from the more relevant feelings I could be paying attention to and addressing. It affects my functioning and productivity at work and leaves me avoiding conversations with friends and family.*	
What do I need in the face of the worry? (Articulating the need with regard to the worry) **Response:** *I need to get a break from my worries.*	
	What do I feel towards the impacted part of me? (Bringing a reminder of compassionate experiences that may help let go of the worry) **Response:** *I feel sad about how much that part of me, impacted by the worrying, has been suffering. I know how strong I am and how much I have endured to get to where I am. When I was little my mum used to help me talk through my worries and help me believe that everything was going to be alright. I want to find ways to be more soothing towards myself, like she was then.*

How can I face the worrying? What points can help me remember how I faced the Worrier in this task and allowed myself to express my emotions?
Response: I can become more aware of when I'm worrying and how it is making me feel so that I can try to respond differently to it. I can be more encouraging of myself and be more accepting that worries are a normal part of my experience, but they don't have to consume me.

An Example of Box 4.3

Summary Sheet: Overcoming Worrying (The Self-Worrier)

Alice's Example: Summary of the Overcoming the Self-Worrier Task

Parts Enacted in the Experiencer-Chair	Parts Enacted in the Worrier-Chair
	How do I worry myself? (Increasing awareness of the ways you worry yourself): **Response:** *Reminding myself of my most feared outcomes such as being exposed as an imposter at work; being rejected by others; and being responsible for ruining my son's future.*
	What drives my worries? (Try to focus on the underlying fears that worrying tries to prevent to be fulfilled) **Response:** *Fear of being abandoned for not being good enough.*
What impact does the worrying have? What is the emotional, physical, and personal cost to me? **Response:** *It caused me to feel stressed and exhausted; tension in my chest; unable to function properly and be productive.*	
What do I need in the face of the worry? (Articulating the need with regard to the worry) **Response:** *I need a break from the worries and to be appreciated for my efforts.*	
	What do I feel towards the impacted part of me? (Bringing a reminder of compassionate experiences that may help let go of the worry) **Response:** *I feel empathy for the impacted part of me. When I was stressed out by my examinations, my grandmother used to remind me to take breaks and drink some soup.*
How can I face the worrying? What points can help me remember how I faced the Worrier in this task and allowed myself to express my emotions? **Response:** *The worrying is the culprit behind my stress and physical ailments. I don't have to listen to the worries. I can take a break from the worries and accept myself for being enough.*	

Answers to the Quiz for Self-Assessment for Chapter 4

		True	False
1	Self-Worrying and Self-Interruption are two types of strategies that people use to avoid their emotions.	☑	☐
2	Feeling tired, exhausted, and anxious are the most typical experiences of persons impacted by Self-Worrying.	☑	☐
3	Worrying often causes us to overprepare for potential threats.	☑	☐
4	Worrying is a form of self-protection against feelings that we do not want to have.	☑	☐
5	Worrying can lead to avoidance of situations that would bring unbearable painful feelings.	☑	☐
6	After completing any experiential task, it can be useful to do the Clearing a Space task or the Compassionate Self-Soothing task.	☑	☐

Appendix V

An Example of Box 5.3

Summary Sheet: Transforming the Self-Critic task

Timothy's Example: Summary of the Transforming the Self-Critic Task

Parts Enacted in the Experiencer-Chair	Parts Enacted in the Critic-Chair
	How do I criticize (attack) myself? (Increasing awareness of the way I treat myself, e.g., criticize, devalue, attack myself, etc.) **Response:** *I tend to beat myself up with words, I undermine myself and my achievements by focusing on everything I feel I've done badly at. I use critical and judgemental language like being a "slob", "pathetic", "not good enough", "stupid", and "failing".*
	What drives my criticism? (e.g., is it a wish to improve myself? A wish to avoid interpersonal judgement and rejection? A wish to earn recognition, respect, love? Or a sense that I deserve to be punished?) **Response:** *I feel like I've always had to work harder than others to be respected and to even just be considered part of the class or the team or whatever. I knew it was my job to help Mum around the house and I think I felt like my helpfulness secured her love as well, which makes me feel like I have to be that way with everyone all the time. My dad leaving has always left a doubt that there was something I did or didn't do to make him go. Maybe I criticize myself with that doubt in mind too like I have a lot to prove and make up for.*
How do I feel when I am being treated like this (criticized, attacked, etc.)? (Reflect on the emotional impact of this which will often be variations of shame or other painful emotions.) **Response:** *It leaves me feeling small and deflated, I usually feel embarrassed or ashamed and like there's no point trying to get out of the situation I'm in. Sometimes I notice feeling this way before I can notice the internal critical dialogue that got me feeling this way in the first place.*	

What do I need when I'm feeling this way/in the face of criticism? (Try to articulate the need stemming from the hurt feelings directed at the critic.)

Response: *I need the critic to accept me as I am. I can't be 100% right all of the time and I need the critic to understand that.*

What do I feel towards the hurt, shamed, put down, vulnerable part of me? (e.g., think about bringing a reminder of the compassionate experiences that may respond to the unmet needs in the vulnerable experience accessed in the Experiencer-Chair.)

Response: *I feel a lot of compassion for that part of me. I feel sorrow for the suffering I've been through. I want it to be different from now on. I know that some days will be easier than others but either way I want to try and notice the pain when it's there rather than spend time and energy distracting myself from it.*

How can I face the Critic? (What will help me remember that I don't have to accept what the Critic says and I can face them and stand up for myself?)

Response: *The critic might want the best for me but the way he goes about it leaves me feeling so miserable and so unable to get on with the things that are important to me. When I think about things fairly or imagine what my best friend would say in response to my doubts or criticisms, I am reminded that I am good enough. I'm not perfect but I'm doing okay and maybe that's all that I can expect of myself. I will say this to the critic (to myself) when I will feel put down by my own critical voice.*

An Example of Box 5.3

Summary Sheet: Transforming the Self-Critic task

Alice's Example: Summary of the Transforming the Self-Critic Task

Parts Enacted in the Experiencer-Chair	Parts Enacted in the Critic-Chair
	How do I criticize (attack) myself? (Increasing awareness of the way I treat myself, e.g., criticize, devalue, attack myself, etc.) **Response:** *I criticize myself for being a bad mother.*
	What drives my criticism? (e.g., is it a wish to improve myself? A wish to avoid interpersonal judgement and rejection? A wish to earn recognition, respect, love? Or a sense that I deserve to be punished?) **Response:** *It is driven by a wish to improve my emotional resilience and also a wish to avoid being hurt or rejected by others.*
How do I feel when I am being treated like this (criticized, attacked, etc.)? (Reflect on the emotional impact of this which will often be variations of shame or other painful emotions.) **Response:** *I feel guilty, sad, hurt, and helpless.*	
What do I need when I'm feeling this way/in the face of criticism? (Try to articulate the need stemming from the hurt feelings and directed at the critic.) **Response:** *I need kindness, gentleness, and compassion. I also need a break from the critic.*	
	What do I feel towards the hurt, shamed, put down, vulnerable part of me? (e.g., think about bringing a reminder of the compassionate experiences that may respond to the unmet needs in the vulnerable experience accessed in the Experiencer-Chair.) **Response:** *I feel tenderness towards the vulnerable part of me. I can remind myself of what my grandmother used to say about my old dog with a limp – "It doesn't have to be perfect to be loved."*
How can I face the Critic? (What will help me remember that I don't have to accept what the Critic says and I can face them and stand up for myself?) **Response:** *I can remind myself that what the Critic says is destructive and I can still grow without undermining my self-worth.*	

Answers to the Quiz for Self-Assessment for Chapter 5

	True	False
1 We often criticize ourselves to improve and be better in our achievements or to improve how we are seen by others.	☑	☐
2 Maladaptive self-criticism can happen when we internalize problematic criticisms directed at us by our authority figures.	☑	☐
3 Self-criticism can elicit feelings of painful shame.	☑	☐
4 We can sometimes begin to actively seek out self-criticism when we start to believe we 'deserve' such self-punishment.	☑	☐
5 The Transforming the Self-Critic task is a form of the 'Self-to-Other' experiential task.	☐	☑
6 Transforming the Self-Critic task seeks to counter shame with emotional experiences such as feeling proud, loved, and appreciated.	☑	☐

Appendix VI

An Example of Box 6.3

Summary Sheet: Transforming Emotional Injury Task

Summary Sheet for Timothy Transforming Interpersonal Emotional Injury Task

Parts Enacted in the Self-Chair	Parts Enacted in the Other-Chair
	What was hurtful in the way the Other was behaving towards me? **Response:** *Dad just acts like nothing ever happened between us. He made the decision to leave, and we never talked about it again. He always makes an effort to be fun and light-hearted when I'm with him, but he never asks me the important questions, like I'm not worth the effort.*
	What was the implied message I heard from them? **Response:** *I feel like I'm just not that important to him. Like he doesn't want to really listen to or understand what it's been like for me growing up, like he doesn't get it and so there's no point trying.*
How do I feel when I am being treated like this? (Note the emotional impact of the Other's behaviour, e.g., loneliness/sadness, shame, fear.) **Response:** *I feel silenced when I'm around him. I feel sad and alone but like there's no point showing this. I try to push these feelings away and just focus on the fact we are getting some time together, but I often feel frustrated or angry afterwards. I think I have a lot to say to him but I'm too afraid that he won't get it or that if I do tell him how I really feel he won't want to spend time with me at all.*	

What do I need when I am/was treated like this from the Other or from somebody else? (Reflect on the unmet need stemming from the hurt feelings and identify to whom this need could be expressed.)

Response: *I need to feel recognized, to be seen and heard by him. I want so badly to be accepted by him and to be absolved of the worry that he just spends time with me out of guilt.*

What do I or the Other (caring part of me or caring part of the Other) feel towards the hurt, vulnerable part of me?

Response: *When I enacted my imagined father, he saw the impact of his behaviour on me and was understanding of it. He felt sorry that it had taken us so long to have the conversation. He wanted me to know that he has always loved me and that it means a lot to him that we've maintained a relationship. It felt great to hear this, validating and reassuring. I felt closer to him, I felt loved, and I felt recognized.*

How can I protect myself if I am treated in this hurtful way again? What was helpful about my current response? (Note down something that will help you remember the sense of resolve you felt during the dialogue)

Response: *This task gave me the courage to try something I never would have done in person. To speak up more about what's on my mind, to take that risk. It felt worth it when the Other person could then understand what it was like for me. It was scary and uncomfortable at first but it was important for me to be able to describe my experience because that made it feel more real, and it helped me to see how the feelings associated with it were justified. I had been holding a lot of these experiences and feelings to myself for a long time.*

An Example of Box 6.3

Summary Sheet: Transforming Emotional Injury Task

Summary Sheet for Alice Transforming Interpersonal Emotional Injury Task

Parts Enacted in the Self-Chair	Parts Enacted in the Other-Chair
	What was hurtful in the way the Other was behaving towards me? **Response:** *I saw my mum implying as if I was a disappointment and not doing anything right at home and with my career.*
	What was the implied message I heard from them? **Response:** *I have enough things on my plate, and I thought I could count on you and would not need to worry about you as well.*
How do I feel when I am being treated like this? (Note the emotional impact of the Other's behaviour, e.g., loneliness/sadness, shame, fear.) **Response:** *I feel ashamed, hurt, and wronged. I feel so small and insignificant, like I don't matter.*	
What do I need when I am/was treated like this from the Other or from somebody else? (Reflect on the unmet need stemming from the hurt feelings and identify to whom this need could be expressed.) **Response:** *I need to be appreciated, loved, and accepted for who I am.*	
	What do I or the Other (caring part of me or caring part of the Other) feel towards the hurt, vulnerable part of me? **Response:** *My caring person is my late grandmother. She is empathetic towards me and she accepts my emotions and needs.*
How can I protect myself if I am treated in this hurtful way again? What was helpful about my current response? (Note down something that will help you remember the sense of resolve you felt during the dialogue.) **Response:** *I can protect myself by keeping an emotional distance from my mum and pursue what I like. I can't change who my mother is but I don't have to let her change me.*	

Answers to the Quiz for Self-Assessment for Chapter 6

	True	False
1 Scaring, burdening, intrusion, and neglect are some of the reasons that can lead to an experience of interpersonal emotional injury.	☑	☐
2 Chronic emotional injuries can occur due to repeated or long-term problematic interactions in both current and/or historic relationships.	☑	☐
3 Emotional injuries usually refer to experiences that generate feelings of sadness only.	☐	☑
4 We can transform emotional injuries by countering them with emotional experiences of self-worrying or self-interruption.	☐	☑
5 We can transform emotional injuries by countering them with experiences of love, compassion, pride, and/or anger.	☑	☐
6 Chronic emotional injuries can severely impact our current relationships by triggering problematic, difficult to process feelings.	☑	☐

Index

Made in the USA
Middletown, DE
13 December 2022

18468825R00106